INSIDE THE OFFICE

Pavithra S Urs | Sanjeev Himachali

notionpress.com

INDIA · SINGAPORE · MALAYSIA

ISBN 979-8-89186-424-5

Contents

Contents

Inception

In the complex fabric of human existence, the common thread uniting us all is the distinct set of beliefs and values that each person carries. These deeply rooted principles serve as the unseen forces that steer us toward our goals and professional ambitions. Nevertheless, to gain a genuine understanding of an individual, one must move beyond the surface and explore the complicated layers of their personal history, education, and life experiences. It is within this complex matrix that an individual's essence takes form, molding their character, driving their motivations, and shaping their aspirations. These layers hold the key to unraveling the enigma of human behavior, granting insight not only into the actions people take but also into the reasons behind them. They provide a glimpse into the rationale and logic that underlie the choices influencing our lives.

In the same vein, organizations also have their unique DNA. They are not random entities but purposefully designed entities, born to address specific issues or challenges in society. At their core, organizations possess a vision and mission that articulate their aspirations and the impact they hope to create. These ambitions are further bolstered by a set of core values that act as guiding stars for every decision and action undertaken within the organization.

The collective beliefs and ethics of an organization meld together to form its distinctive culture, an invisible force that attracts talent and nurtures an environment where individuals can flourish. This organizational culture sets one entity apart from another, providing it with a unique identity.

Imagine the dynamic interplay when individuals, each with their own unique blend of beliefs, values, backgrounds, and aspirations, converge with an organization steeped in its distinct vision, culture, and core values. The result is akin to alchemy. The fusion of individual and organizational uniqueness generates a rich series of experiences, a symphony of perspectives, and a trove of invaluable lessons.

In the chronicles of our professional journey, both Sanjeev and I have been fortunate to traverse the landscape of diversity. We've had the privilege of working with culturally diverse groups, learning profound lessons along the way. The tales in this book are not just personal anecdotes but are representative of the collective experiences shared within our professional network. This book is our endeavor to collect and curate these experiences, presenting them as stories and insights for the next generation of aspiring managers.

These stories are not conjured from thin air; they are born from the crucible of reality. They are the result of encounters, challenges, and triumphs experienced by either one of us or by individuals within our professional circle. Each story is a testament to the idea that experiences are stories, and stories are lessons. The wisdom gained from these experiences has not only shaped our professional lives but also provided a guiding light, illuminating our paths in our careers.

In this book, we aim to convey the essence of these experiences. Each narrative unfolds as a learning story, revealing the richness of the lessons we've encountered. As we delve into each experience, we aim to unveil the underlying principles and insights that can guide young managers on their journey. These experiences have served as our mentors, teaching us the art of making the right choices and the wisdom to discern the right decisions.

But why should these stories matter to young managers and emerging leaders? What is the significance of sharing these experiences with a new generation of professionals? The answer lies in the transformative power of stories.

Stories are not mere narratives; they are mirrors reflecting the essence of human experiences. They possess the power to inspire, to connect, and to impart knowledge. As young managers set foot on their career paths, they do so with dreams and aspirations but also with trepidation, the natural uncertainty that accompanies new beginnings.

It's at this juncture that stories become their guiding light. Through stories, young managers can learn about the real-world challenges and triumphs of those who have walked similar paths before them. These stories offer solace, letting them know they are not alone in their struggles and celebrations. The wisdom distilled from experiences shared in stories serves as a lighthouse, guiding them safely through the labyrinth of professional life.

The relevance of these stories lies in their universality. They transcend time, culture, and borders. The experiences shared in this book are not bound by a particular time or place; they are lessons drawn from the very fabric of human interactions, challenges, and accomplishments. Thus, regardless of one's background or unique circumstances, the lessons in these stories are applicable to a diverse array of professional situations.

This book is a meticulously crafted treasure chest, overflowing with experiences, lessons, and insights, meant to be shared with those embarking on their journey as managers and leaders. It is a testament to the idea that knowledge, when shared, becomes a legacy. As we pass the torch to the next generation of managers, we are not just imparting knowledge but also the wisdom to navigate the intricate web of the professional world. These stories, our experiences, are not just tales of success or failure but a compendium of strategies, insights, and principles that can serve as guideposts in the journey ahead.

We invite you to dive into this treasure trove of experiences, for within these stories, you may discover the keys to unlocking your own potential and achieving your aspirations. These experiences have shaped us, and we are confident they will shape you too, inspiring you to make the right choices and to make the right decisions as you navigate the multifaceted world of management and leadership.

Organizational DNA – Culture & Core Values

1. The Empathetic Edge: Outplacement & Employer Branding

In the rapidly evolving landscape of modern businesses, the way companies treat their employees during challenging times speaks volumes about their true character and values. While downsizing and restructuring may be necessary for survival, it is how an organization navigates such transitions that truly sets it apart as an employer of choice. **Enter the transformative force of outplacement—a powerful tool that, when harnessed efficiently, can revolutionize an organization's employer branding efforts.**

In this age of talent scarcity and fierce competition for top-notch professionals, companies must go beyond mere promises and showcase genuine empathy in action. By prioritizing the welfare of departing employees and offering them a lifeline during times of change, a company can pave the way to an unmatched employer brand. This article unravels the intricacies of outplacement and unveils how its thoughtful implementation can reverberate throughout an organization, leaving an indelible mark on its reputation and shaping the course of its success.

Join us on a journey to discover how outplacement, when embraced with authenticity and care, can kindle the flames of employee loyalty, foster a supportive and motivated workforce, and capture the attention of the industry's finest talents. **Through real-life case studies and expert insights, we'll explore how outplacement not only helps departing employees find their footing in new horizons but also becomes the bedrock of a company's identity as an ethical, compassionate, and future-focused employer.**

Once upon a time, in the vibrant city of Mumbai, there was a prominent software company named "TechSolutions India." For years, it has been at the forefront of technological innovation, serving clients worldwide. However, the global economic downturn brought unforeseen challenges, forcing TechSolutions India to reevaluate its operations.

With a heavy heart, the company's leadership had to make the difficult decision of downsizing a significant portion of its workforce. Faced with this daunting task, they knew that their approach had to be empathetic and supportive. TechSolutions India decided to partner with "EmpowerNext," a renowned outplacement firm that specializes in providing comprehensive assistance to employees transitioning out of their jobs. **EmpowerNext was well-known for its success stories of helping individuals navigate through career changes with renewed confidence.**

As the day of the layoffs approached, the atmosphere in TechSolutions India was tense. However, the HR team worked hand in hand with EmpowerNext to ensure that the departing employees received the utmost care and support. One of the affected employees, Rajesh, has been with TechSolutions India since its inception. He felt shattered and uncertain about his future. However, the outplacement services from Empower Next came as a ray of hope. They offered Rajesh **career guidance, resume building, and personalized coaching sessions.**

In the months that followed, TechSolutions India focused on streamlining its operations and adapting to the changing market demands. Meanwhile, Rajesh utilized the support from EmpowerNext to explore new career avenues. With EmpowerNext's guidance, Rajesh discovered his passion for teaching and sharing his technical knowledge with aspiring young minds. He pursued certification in education and soon found himself as a respected faculty member at a prestigious engineering college in Mumbai.

As news of TechSolutions India's compassionate approach to layoffs spread, the company's reputation grew exponentially. Job seekers admired the company's commitment to supporting its employees during difficult times, and the best talents were drawn to join its workforce.

TechSolutions India transformed the challenges of the economic downturn into an opportunity for growth and strengthened their brand. The company's core values of empathy and care became its defining features, earning it recognition as an employer of choice in the Indian tech industry.

BENEFITS OF OUTPLACEMENT SERVICES

1. **Employee Loyalty and Morale**: Outplacement programs demonstrate that employers genuinely care about their employees, even during challenging times such as downsizing or restructuring. By offering support and assistance to departing employees, companies foster a sense of loyalty and trust among their workforce. This approach shows that the organization

values its employees as more than just mere assets but as individuals with real-life concerns and aspirations.

When employees feel that their well-being is a priority, they are more likely to have positive feelings toward the company, even after their departure. This positivity can manifest in the form of maintaining friendly relationships with former colleagues, endorsing the company on professional platforms, and speaking favorably about their experiences working there.

2. **Positive Word-of-Mouth**: Outplacement services can lead to positive word-of-mouth referrals, which is a powerful form of employer branding. When employees experience a supportive exit process, they are more inclined to share their experiences with friends, family, and professional networks.

   Positive testimonials from former employees can resonate strongly with potential candidates. Job seekers are increasingly researching company cultures and employee experiences before deciding where to apply. Hearing about a company's commitment to supporting its employees during transitions can be a significant factor in attracting top talent.

3. **Alignment with Company Values**: Incorporating outplacement services into an organization's practices aligns with its core values. Companies that prioritize employee welfare, even during difficult times, demonstrate integrity and empathy, essential qualities in an employer. This alignment with values creates a stronger sense of purpose and identity for the organization.

   When a company's actions align with its stated values, it enhances the perception of the organization as authentic and trustworthy. Prospective employees are more likely to be drawn to a company with a strong sense of purpose and a demonstrated commitment to its values.

4. **Impact on Remaining Employees**: The way an organization handles employee transitions can significantly influence the morale and motivation of the remaining workforce. Downsizing or layoffs can create fear and uncertainty among employees who are still with the company.

   Offering outplacement services signals to the remaining employees that the organization cares about its people and is willing to support them through challenging times. This can boost the morale of the remaining workforce and foster a positive work environment. When employees feel valued and supported, they are more likely to be engaged, productive, and committed to the organization.

5. **Attracting Top Talent:** As competition for top talent intensifies, companies must find innovative ways to differentiate themselves as employers of choice. The provision of outplacement services can give organizations a competitive advantage in attracting skilled and experienced professionals.

   Job seekers consider a company's reputation and employer brand when evaluating potential employers. An organization known for its commitment to employee well-being, even in difficult situations, will stand out as an attractive option for top talent. This can lead to a larger pool of qualified candidates and better retention rates in the long run.

6. **Mitigating Negative Publicity**: Downsizing or layoffs can sometimes attract negative attention in the media and on social platforms. Companies that neglect to offer outplacement

support risk facing public backlash and damage to their reputation.

On the other hand, organizations that proactively provide outplacement services demonstrate responsible and ethical practices. By taking care of their departing employees, they show that they are committed to doing the right thing, even when faced with difficult decisions. This proactive approach can mitigate negative publicity and help preserve the company's image.

7. **Retaining Positive Relationships with Alumni**: Former employees can remain valuable assets to an organization even after they leave. They can act as brand ambassadors, provide referrals for potential employees, or even become future business partners or clients.

By providing outplacement services, a company maintains a positive relationship with its alumni. Departing employees who receive support during their transition are more likely to remain positively connected to the organization. This connection can open doors for potential collaborations and partnerships in the future.

As we reach the culmination of our exploration into the world of outplacement and its profound impact on employer branding, a resounding truth emerges: **empathy is the delicate thread that weaves together the fabric of a legendary employer brand.** Just as a master craftsman artfully blends color and textures to create a mesmerizing tapestry, so too does a compassionate organization infuse its core with the hues of understanding, care, and support.

We have witnessed how the ripple effect of outplacement can transform the corporate landscape, transcending the realm of mere HR practices. Like a beacon of hope in a sea of uncertainty, **outplacement offers departing employees the lifeline they need to embark on new adventures, nurturing loyalty and leaving an indelible mark on their hearts.**

So, as we bid adieu to our journey through the realms of outplacement and employer branding, let us carry forth the lessons learned and the spirit of empathy instilled. In this vast cosmos of interconnected experiences, let us remember that every interaction, every gesture of kindness, shapes the destiny of an employer brand.

Let us be the architects of a new era where empathy is not a fleeting concept but a guiding principle—a North Star illuminating the path to organizational greatness. Together, we shall unravel the enigma of outplacement, transforming it into a symphony of harmony and prosperity, leaving a resonating echo that inspires generations to come.

With empathy at its core, an employer brand transcends the ordinary, painting a masterpiece in the annals of corporate history—a masterpiece adorned not with mere accomplishments but with the heartfelt stories of lives touched, dreams realized, and a legacy of compassion woven into the very fabric of its existence.

2. Beyond Resumes: Decoding the Challenges of Hiring Senior Executives

Selecting the right senior executive is a crucial decision that can shape the trajectory of an organization. These high-level roles demand individuals with the vision, experience, and leadership prowess to drive growth, inspire teams, and steer the company toward success. However, the path to finding these exceptional leaders is fraught with challenges. Limited opportunities, an abundance of qualified applicants, the quest for the ideal candidate, and the need to balance technical expertise with soft skills all contribute to the complexity of the senior executive hiring process.

In this article, we delve into the multifaceted challenges faced by organizations in hiring senior executives and explore strategies to overcome them. We will uncover the intricacies of identifying the right candidate, evaluating their cultural fit, mitigating bias, and embracing diversity. By understanding and addressing these challenges head-on, organizations can position themselves for success by assembling high-performing leadership teams that drive innovation, foster a positive company culture, and navigate the ever-changing business landscape with confidence.

Join us as we embark on a journey through the intricacies of hiring senior executives, where limited opportunities are met with an abundance of applicants and organizations strive to find the perfect balance between qualifications, soft skills, cultural fit, and diversity. Together, we will explore the strategies and approaches that can unlock the door to exceptional leadership, enabling organizations to thrive in a competitive and dynamic business environment.

LIMITED OPPORTUNITIES, ABUNDANT APPLICANTS

At the senior executive level, job opportunities are relatively scarce compared to lower-level positions. As professionals progress in their careers and reach mid- to senior-level positions, the number of available positions becomes increasingly limited. This scarcity creates a high demand for these top-tier roles, attracting a multitude of highly qualified applicants. With a surplus of candidates competing for a select few positions, organizations face the difficult task of identifying the most suitable candidate who possesses the necessary qualifications, experience, and leadership qualities.

To effectively navigate this challenge, organizations often employ strategic talent acquisition techniques. They may leverage their networks, industry connections, and executive search firms to identify potential candidates. Additionally, organizations may create comprehensive job descriptions and requirements that clearly outline the skills and experience they seek. By setting clear expectations and casting a wide net, organizations can increase their chances of attracting qualified applicants and finding the best fit for the role.

THE QUEST FOR THE IDEAL CANDIDATE

Finding the ideal candidate for a senior executive role is a complex undertaking. These positions require a unique blend of skills, expertise, and leadership capabilities. Organizations seek individuals who can navigate complex business landscapes, drive growth, and provide strategic vision. Identifying an individual who possesses this rare combination can be a daunting challenge.

To overcome this challenge, organizations often implement a rigorous screening process. This may involve multiple rounds of interviews with various stakeholders, including executives, board members, and key team members. Assessments and simulations may be conducted to evaluate a candidate's decision-making abilities, problem-solving skills, and leadership style. Additionally, thorough background checks, including reference checks and verification of past accomplishments, help organizations gain a comprehensive understanding of a candidate's qualifications and suitability for the role.

BALANCING TECHNICAL AND SOFT SKILLS

Senior executive positions require a delicate balance between technical expertise and soft skills. While technical proficiency is crucial in guiding strategic decision-making, understanding industry dynamics, and driving innovation, it is the soft skills that truly differentiate exceptional leaders. Strong communication, emotional intelligence, adaptability, and the ability to inspire and motivate teams are essential qualities that senior executives must possess.

To assess both technical and soft skills, organizations employ a range of evaluation methods. Traditional interviews may be supplemented with behavioral-based questions that require candidates to provide specific examples of their past experiences and demonstrate their soft skills in action. Additionally, situational assessments or case studies may be used to gauge a candidate's ability to think critically and make sound decisions under pressure. By utilizing a combination of assessment tools, organizations can obtain a holistic view of a candidate's capabilities and potential fit for the role.

CULTURE FIT AND ORGANIZATIONAL ALIGNMENT

In addition to qualifications and skills, cultural fit and alignment with the organization's values and vision play a pivotal role in selecting senior executives. These leaders are tasked with shaping the company's culture, driving change, and aligning teams toward common goals. Therefore, finding candidates who resonate with the organization's culture is crucial for seamless integration and long-term success.

To evaluate culture fit, organizations may incorporate behavioral and values-based interview questions that assess a candidate's alignment with the company's core values and cultural norms. Additionally, culture assessments or exercises may be conducted to gauge how well a candidate's work style, communication approach, and leadership philosophy align with the organization's culture. By involving key stakeholders in the hiring process, such as employees who will directly interact with the senior executive, organizations can gain valuable insights into a candidate's potential fit within the existing team dynamics.

MITIGATING BIAS AND EMBRACING DIVERSITY

Addressing bias and promoting diversity in senior executive hiring is an ongoing challenge for organizations. Unconscious biases, such as affinity bias or confirmation bias, can inadvertently influence decision-making, leading to a lack of diversity in leadership positions.

To mitigate bias and promote diversity, organizations are taking proactive steps to create fair and inclusive hiring processes. This includes adopting blind resume screenings, where identifying information such as names and educational institutions is removed from resumes to reduce bias. Diverse interview panels are formed to offer multiple perspectives and reduce the influence of individual biases. Structured interview questions and evaluation criteria are used to ensure consistency and fairness in assessing candidates. Organizations may also implement diversity and inclusion training programs to raise awareness and sensitivity among hiring teams.

As organizations seek to fill senior executive positions, they must recognize that it is not only about finding someone with the right qualifications and experience but also about identifying individuals who possess the vision, passion, and leadership qualities necessary to steer the organization to new heights. By investing time, resources, and innovative strategies in the hiring process, organizations can increase their chances of identifying exceptional leaders who will shape the future of the company.

The road to finding the right senior executive may be filled with challenges, but the rewards of selecting the right candidate are immeasurable. These leaders have the potential to transform organizations, drive growth, and inspire teams to achieve greatness. By overcoming the limitations of limited opportunities, mitigating bias, and embracing diversity, organizations can build robust leadership teams that possess the knowledge, skills, and passion to navigate the complexities of the business world.

As the business landscape continues to evolve, the importance of hiring the right senior executives becomes even more pronounced. Organizations that adapt to changing dynamics, leverage innovative assessment methods, and prioritize cultural fit and diversity will position themselves at the forefront of success. By recognizing the significance of these challenges and implementing effective strategies to address them, organizations can secure their future by selecting leaders who possess not only the right pedigree but also the vision and passion necessary to thrive in an ever-changing business landscape.

In the pursuit of excellence, organizations must rise to the occasion and embrace the complexities and challenges that come with hiring senior executives. By doing so, they will unlock the potential for transformative leadership, ensuring long-term success and sustainable growth in an increasingly competitive and dynamic business environment.

3. Beyond Boundaries: The Maverick Manager Who Revolutionized Talent Acquisition

In the bustling heart of Mumbai, India, the world of software development saw a managerial legend emerge: Rajesh, a leader who demonstrated unwavering commitment to the art of talent acquisition. Rajesh was no ordinary manager; he stood at the helm of a dynamic team in one of India's premier software development companies, shouldering a multitude of responsibilities. Among these responsibilities, one stood out as his true calling: recruitment.

To Rajesh, recruitment was not a mere checkbox on his task list; it was a mission. When the word "recruitment" appeared on his agenda, it instantly became his top priority, overshadowing all other responsibilities. The pursuit of identifying and hiring the right individuals for his team and, in effect, for the entire organization became an unwavering focus.

This unparalleled dedication often led Rajesh to push the boundaries of conventional work hours. He was not a manager who adhered strictly to the confines of the 9-to-5 workday. He recognized that exceptional talent often operated on their own schedules. Thus, if conducting interviews late into the night or even on weekends was the means to discover hidden gems, Rajesh embraced this unconventional path with open arms.

For Rajesh, recruitment went beyond the ordinary; it transcended the conventional norms. He often repeated the mantra, "Few things go beyond normal, and talent search is one such thing." Rajesh understood that following the well-trodden path of other hiring managers would only yield predictable results. To attract top-tier talent, he needed to be innovative and daring in his approach.

Embedded in Rajesh's philosophy was the belief that "If you want to get what is not easily available, then you must also be willing to do what you normally do not do." This principle became his guiding light, not just in talent acquisition but in every facet of his work. He realized that extraordinary talent seldom resided in conventional channels, and uncovering it required taking unconventional measures.

Rajesh's commitment to recruitment wasn't just a personal quest; it was a message that resonated throughout the organization. His actions spoke louder than words, illustrating his deep reverence for the value of talent. This unwavering dedication didn't just attract exceptional candidates; it inspired unwavering commitment and loyalty from his team members. They were moved by Rajesh's relentless pursuit of excellence.

With time, Rajesh's approach permeated the culture within the company. It was no longer just about identifying the right individuals; it was about fostering an environment where talent was not merely valued but celebrated. Rajesh's team members didn't just see him as a manager; they viewed him as a mentor who embodied the idea that going beyond normal was the path to extraordinary achievements.

Nonetheless, Rajesh's unconventional methods came with their fair share of challenges. In an industry where interviews were typically conducted during regular working hours and weekends were off-limits, his peers often viewed his approach with skepticism. They questioned his decision to reschedule interviews and seek out candidates through unconventional routes.

A recurring criticism was, "We don't have enough resources to complete our projects on time." Some argued that Rajesh's emphasis on recruitment was causing project delays. Rajesh, however, had a different perspective. He firmly believed that the caliber of talent he brought to the team would lead to superior project outcomes. Any momentary disruptions were seen as a worthwhile investment in the organization's long-term success.

As the years passed, Rajesh's reputation as a hiring manager willing to go to great lengths to secure top talent continued to grow. He became renowned not just within his organization but across the industry. Job seekers aspired to work with him, and his peers held him in high regard. His story served as an inspirational beacon, illustrating that going beyond normal in the pursuit of talent could lead to remarkable results.

One fateful day, as Rajesh perused his emails, one message stood out. It was from a promising young software engineer named Aarti. She had heard about Rajesh's unconventional recruitment approach and admired his dedication to finding exceptional talent. Aarti believed she possessed the skills and passion to make a meaningful contribution to Rajesh's team.

Impressed by Aarti's message and her outstanding portfolio, Rajesh decided to schedule an interview with her. However, there was a twist: Aarti was currently immersed in a project that kept her occupied during regular working hours for the next few weeks. The only available window for an interview was on a Sunday, a day that Rajesh typically reserved for personal time and rest.

Without hesitation, Rajesh agreed to the Sunday interview. He understood that exceptional talent often operated on unconventional schedules, and he was more than willing to accommodate. When Aarti arrived for the interview on that Sunday morning, she was taken aback to find Rajesh waiting in his office. She had expected that he might delegate the interview or conduct it remotely, but Rajesh's commitment to the process left a profound impression on her.

The interview proceeded remarkably well, and it was evident to both Rajesh and Aarti that they had discovered a perfect match. Aarti's technical prowess was nothing short of exceptional, and her fervor for software development mirrored Rajesh's passion for talent recruitment. At the interview's conclusion, Rajesh extended an offer to Aarti to join his team, an offer she enthusiastically accepted.

As Aarti integrated into her new role, she discovered that Rajesh's commitment to talent acquisition extended far beyond the recruitment process. He was a mentor and a leader who believed in nurturing and developing the potential of each team member. Under Rajesh's guidance, Aarti thrived, and her contributions to the team became invaluable.

Word of Aarti's success quickly spread throughout the organization. Her story served as a testament to Rajesh's unique approach to recruitment and management. It wasn't just about finding talent; it was about recognizing potential and creating an environment where individuals could flourish and excel.

Over time, more team members followed in Aarti's footsteps, joining Rajesh's team not merely for the exciting projects but because they sought to be part of a culture that cherished talent and innovation above all else. Rajesh had successfully cultivated a culture where every team member felt like a vital asset and where going beyond normal was not just encouraged but expected.

As Rajesh's team continued to flourish and evolve, so did the organization as a whole. Their innovative solutions and exceptional work attracted more clients and projects, propelling the company to new pinnacles of success. Rajesh's relentless commitment to talent acquisition had not only transformed his team but had a cascading impact that reverberated throughout the entire organization.

Rajesh's narrative metamorphosed into a legend in the realms of recruitment and management. He was not merely a manager; he was a trailblazer who had demonstrated that the pursuit of excellence in talent acquisition could lead to extraordinary triumphs. His story served as a wellspring of inspiration for hiring managers and leaders, not only in India but across the globe.

Ultimately, Rajesh's journey underscored the profound truth that, in the pursuit of extraordinary talent, one must transcend the boundaries of convention. To uncover what is not easily attainable, one must be willing to embark on unconventional paths. Rajesh's legacy was more than just finding the right people; it was about crafting a culture where talent was not merely revered but exalted, where going beyond normal was not merely a choice but a way of life, and where excellence was not just a goal but a state of being. Rajesh's remarkable tale continues to inspire us all to reach beyond the ordinary in our quest for excellence.

4. Impact of Psychometric Assessments on Making Right Hiring Decisions

The cost of incorrect decision-making during the recruitment process is something that every organization tries to minimize. Psychometric assessment serves the very purpose of an organization. Theoretically, psychometrics is the measurement of the mind—the measurement of behavioral traits and personality, to be precise.

While the traditional methods of hiring are doing fairly well in shortlisting the employees with the best skillset, Experience, intelligence, critical reasoning, motivation, and personality profile are the aspects that are often left uncovered. This is where psychometric assessments come into play.

WHY USE PSYCHOMETRIC ASSESSMENTS?

At present, only 18% of the companies are using psychometric assessments in their respective hiring processes, as per a survey performed by the Society for Human Resource Management. The agenda of psychometric assessments is to provide the company with measurable, objective data that will help them assess the credibility of the applicants.

It tends to reduce the workload of the HR manager by restricting the pool of applicants to a smaller one who has cleared some predefined standardized tests. That may contain numerical, graphical, or verbal challenges.

HOW DO I USE PSYCHOMETRIC ASSESSMENT?

Before moving on with the implementation of psychometric assessments, an organization should have a glance at the following aspects to cut short the potential risks:

LOOK FOR THE PROVISIONS OF THE CONCERNING LAW

While adding psychometric assessments to the hiring process, keep in mind regulatory compliance. Ensure adherence to anti-discrimination laws. The methods of assessment need to be closely related to the job. For example, in America, the Disabilities Act prohibits impairment of any sort of diagnosis for such people.

ASSESS BUSINESS NEEDS

A sound psychometric assessment process may not be effective if it does not evaluate the characteristics most desired for the company. The focus of the organization should be more on "dependent variables" than on "independent variables" to obtain precise results.

SHARE THE TEST RESULTS WITH THE APPLICANTS

The principle of "informed consent" gives the applicants a right to access their performance results. Even though it's not a compulsion, an organization is expected to adopt this practice on ethical and moral grounds.

THE MOST SOUGHT-AFTER PSYCHOMETRIC ASSESSMENT TESTS

- Sixteen **Personality Factor Questionnaires:**

  As evident from the name itself, it emphasizes 16 personality traits. This test is devised to determine how an employee will react when subjected to certain conditions. This test might contain up to 170 questions, depending on the complexity of the job posting and the skill requirements.

- **Personality profiling:**

  Usually, this is the first step in the recruitment process, though it is not a compulsion. This test is used to detect whether potential employees have the desired attributes and skills for a particular job or not. There are no absolute right or wrong answers to the questions asked under this test; what they look for is the attitude of the potential employees toward these questions.

- **DISC:**

  It is again a tool that helps in assessing the personalities of the applicants. DISC was devised by industrial psychologist Walter Vernon Clarke. DISC is concerned with the evaluation of these four behavioral traits: dominance, inducement, submission, and compliance. It is also directed toward the identification of leadership qualities.

- Numerical **Reasoning Assessment:**

  This test aims at interpreting the individual's ability to deal with numerical data. To check the compatibility of the candidate when subjected to numerical data in the form of graphs and charts. Note that it is not aimed at measuring the mathematical skills of a candidate; it is to analyze how handy or comfortable a candidate is with numerical data.

IMPACT OF PSYCHOMETRIC ASSESSMENTS ON HIRING DECISIONS

- The most sought-after takeaway from the use of psychometric assessment is that it renders results that can be relied upon with an ample amount of confidence. Different job positions require different attributes, and personal interviews might not fulfill the needs each time around.

- It is cost-effective in the long run. This statement might appear exaggerated to many people, as the initial installation expenses of deploying psychometric assessment techniques into the recruitment process consume a lot of money. But in the long run, it lowers the cost of gathering essential information about potential employees. It can perform the task in hours, which might consume days of HR personnel. It lowers the cost of poor performance and a high employee turnover ratio significantly.

- Personal bias is hard to resist during personal interviews. Bias will pop up, whether knowingly or unknowingly. Psychometric assessments address the problem of bias conveniently; tests care little about the connections of the applicant with the management or the age, religion, sex, etc. of the candidate.

- Such tests increase the selection speed exponentially. For an organization that might receive thousands of applications, psychometric assessments prove to be of great help in filtering out candidates who aren't worthy of the positions they applied for.

- Subjecting the applicants to such tests will ensure their seriousness for the job post. Completing a test takes a great deal of time and skills, of course, so if an applicant is attempting the test, it is an indicator of his commitment to the job. As a result of this test, only dedicated applicants will proceed further.

- On the management front, psychometric assessments help managers gain meaningful insights about the learning styles, preferred working styles, behaviors, and motivations at work of the candidates.

Moreover, psychometric assessments have proven their worth in imparting successful placements. It can be taken as a big takeaway that it enhances compatibility to a great extent within and across teams inside the organization. Organizations that have implemented such tests have a positive employee retention ratio and reduced probation. Since the tests are based on facts and figures, there's no place for unconscious bias.

5. The Art of Recruitment: Managing Ghosting with Compassion

In the heart of Mumbai, a city that never slept, a small IT startup named InnoTech Solutions was on the cusp of something big. The company had developed cutting-edge software solutions that promised to revolutionize the industry. However, there was one significant challenge they faced that threatened to disrupt their progress: candidates ghosting their prospective employers.

The problem had become alarmingly common. Promising interviews would be scheduled, but candidates would simply vanish into thin air, leaving the HR team baffled and frustrated. Meera, the Head of HR at InnoTech Solutions, was determined to find a solution to this perplexing issue.

One Monday morning, as the sun rose over the sprawling metropolis, Meera gathered her team in the cozy conference room at InnoTech's office. She could see the frustration etched on their faces. "I know we've been facing a recurring problem lately," she began, "but we're not alone in this. Many companies are grappling with candidates ghosting during the recruitment process."

Meera continued, "We can't control the actions of candidates, but we can control how we respond to this challenge. We need to find a way to manage candidates who ghost and ensure that our recruitment process remains smooth and efficient."

THE STRATEGIES UNVEILED

Meera had a plan. She had researched and formulated a set of strategies to tackle the ghosting issue head-on. As she addressed her team, she shared her vision.

Here are the strategies we're going to implement to manage candidates who ghost:

- Follow-up regularly: We'll start by sending candidates reminders about scheduled interviews or deadlines. After each interview, we'll follow-up with them, expressing our continued interest and asking for feedback.

- Provide clear communication: Clear and transparent communication is key. We need to lay out expectations, timelines, and the next steps of the recruitment process during the initial stages. This will help candidates understand the significance of their role in the process.

- Be respectful: Candidates may have valid reasons for ghosting. It could be personal issues, unexpected changes in their lives, or a loss of interest. Regardless of the reason, we must maintain a respectful and positive relationship with every candidate.

- Consider automation: To streamline our efforts, we'll invest in advanced recruitment software that can automate reminders and follow-ups. This will significantly reduce the number of candidates who ghost, as they'll receive regular, automated reminders about their interviews and next steps.

- Keep a pipeline of candidates: We should always have a pipeline of potential candidates ready. This way, if a candidate ghosts, we can swiftly move on to the next one without wasting too much time and effort.

- Evaluate the recruitment process: Let's conduct a thorough assessment of our recruitment process. We need to identify areas that could be improved, such as speeding up the decision-making process and making the candidate experience more engaging and informative."

The team nodded in agreement, inspired by Meera's determination and the clarity of her plan. They were ready to embark on this journey to transform their recruitment process.

IMPLEMENTING THE STRATEGIES

With the strategies in place, the HR team at InnoTech Solutions started their mission to combat ghost candidates. It was not an easy task, but they were determined to make it work.

1. Follow-Up Regularly: The first step was to implement regular follow-ups. As interviews were scheduled, candidates began receiving reminders via email and text messages. These reminders were polite and professional, ensuring candidates felt valued and respected.

   After each interview, Meera's team made it a point to follow-up promptly. They sent personalized emails, expressing their appreciation for the candidate's time and their interest in joining InnoTech Solutions. This simple act of courtesy went a long way in making candidates feel acknowledged and valued.

2. Providing Clear Communication: Clear communication was the linchpin of InnoTech's strategy. Meera's team revamped their initial interactions with candidates. They created informative and engaging recruitment brochures that outlined the company's culture, values, and expectations. This allowed candidates to have a clearer understanding of what they were getting into.

   During interviews, the HR team made sure to explain the entire recruitment process, including expected timelines and the steps that candidates would go through. This transparency helped candidates comprehend the importance of their role in the process and set realistic expectations.

3. Being Respectful: The HR team at InnoTech Solutions took Meera's advice to heart and decided to be respectful, regardless of the situation. Candidates who had ghosted in the past were approached with a considerate tone. Meera encouraged her team to consider the possibility that candidates might be facing personal issues or unexpected changes in their lives.

   One day, as the team was following up with a candidate named Priya who had ghosted after the initial interview, they received an email response. Priya apologized profusely for her absence and explained that she had experienced a family emergency. She thanked InnoTech's team for their understanding and patience.

Meera was moved by Priya's email. She replied promptly, expressing her sympathy and offering support. While Priya ultimately decided not to continue with the recruitment process due to her family's ongoing situation, she left with a positive impression of InnoTech Solutions and even recommended the company to her network.

1. Considering Automation: The automation aspect was a game-changer. InnoTech Solutions invested in cutting-edge recruitment software that automates reminders and follow-ups. This not only saved time but also ensured that no candidate slipped through the cracks.

Candidates received automated reminders about upcoming interviews, deadlines for submitting documents, and even follow-up emails post-interview. This systematic approach reduced the chances of candidates forgetting about their commitments and thus reduced ghosting incidents significantly.

1. Keeping a Pipeline of Candidates: To ensure they could swiftly move on to the next candidate if someone ghosted, InnoTech Solutions built a robust pipeline of potential candidates. This was a proactive approach to minimize disruptions caused by ghosting incidents.

2. The team established partnerships with local universities and attended job fairs regularly to maintain a steady flow of talent into their pipeline. This approach not only provided them with a pool of candidates to choose from but also increased their visibility in the job market.

3. Evaluating the Recruitment Process: In the midst of implementing these strategies, the HR team at InnoTech Solutions also dedicated time to evaluating their recruitment process. They conducted surveys among candidates who had completed interviews and gathered valuable feedback.

One of the candidates, Rajesh, who had recently joined the company, shared his insights. He praised the clear communication and respectful follow-ups. Rajesh pointed out that these aspects had played a significant role in his decision to accept the job offer.

Meera's team took this feedback seriously. They identified areas where they could further improve, such as providing more detailed information about the company's projects and career growth opportunities. These improvements made the recruitment process even more engaging and informative.

THE IMPACT UNFOLDS

As weeks turned into months, the impact of InnoTech Solutions' strategies began to unfold. The number of candidates who ghosted dropped significantly. Meera and her team were no longer chasing shadows but rather engaging with candidates who were genuinely interested in joining the company.

THE CASE OF ARJUN

One day, a candidate named Arjun walked into the InnoTech Solutions office for an interview. He was a highly qualified professional with an impressive resume, and he seemed genuinely enthusiastic about the position.

The interview went well, and the HR team, true to their strategy, followed up with Arjun promptly. However, days turned into weeks, and there was no response from him. Meera was about to mark him as another ghosted candidate when she received an email from Arjun.

In his email, Arjun apologized for the delay and explained that he had faced a family emergency that required his immediate attention. He expressed his gratitude for the patience and respect shown by InnoTech Solutions during the process. Meera, touched by his honesty, replied, assuring him that they understood his situation and would be ready to continue the process when he was ready.

Months later, Arjun joined InnoTech Solutions as a valuable team member. He often mentioned how the respectful and considerate approach of the HR team during his family crisis had made a lasting impression on him. This incident highlighted the importance of maintaining a compassionate and understanding attitude toward candidates.

BUILDING A REPUTATION

InnoTech Solutions not only improved its recruitment process but also built a reputation for being a compassionate and understanding employer in the competitive world of Mumbai's tech startups. Word spread in the industry about their respectful approach, and talented candidates began seeking out opportunities with the company.

Meera and her team continued to recruit top talent, armed with a newfound understanding of the power of patience and respectful communication. They were no longer haunted by ghosting candidates, and their recruitment process had become a smooth and efficient operation.

LESSONS LEARNED

As time passed, InnoTech Solutions continued to thrive, and the HR team learned valuable lessons from their journey to manage candidates who ghosted. Here are some of the key takeaways:

- Respect and Compassion Go a Long Way: Treating candidates with respect and understanding, even in the face of ghosting, can leave a positive and lasting impression. Candidates appreciate it when recruiters acknowledge their circumstances and maintain a respectful attitude.

- Clear Communication is Essential. Clear and transparent communication is the foundation of any successful recruitment process. Providing candidates with detailed information about the company, the role, and the recruitment process helps manage expectations and reduce ghosting incidents.

- Automation Enhances Efficiency: Investing in automation tools can significantly enhance the efficiency of the recruitment process. Automated reminders and follow-ups ensure that candidates stay engaged and informed throughout the process.

- Continuous Improvement is Key. Evaluating the recruitment process regularly and seeking feedback from candidates can lead to continuous improvement. It allows organizations to fine-tune their approach and create a more engaging and informative candidate experience.

A Bright Future: InnoTech Solutions successfully managed candidates who ghosted by implementing a well-thought-out set of strategies. They had not only improved their recruitment process but had also established a reputation as an employer that cared about its candidates.

As the Mumbai skyline glittered with the lights of progress, InnoTech Solutions continued to grow, attracting top talent from across the country. The challenge of candidate ghosting was no longer a daunting obstacle but a reminder of the company's commitment to respectful and compassionate recruitment practices.

Meera, the head of HR, looked out of her office window, reflecting on the journey they had undertaken. She knew that their success was not just about finding the right candidates; it was also about treating every individual with dignity and respect. In the dynamic world of tech startups, InnoTech Solutions had carved a niche for itself as an organization that valued people as much as technology.

As they looked to the future, they did so with confidence, knowing that the strategies they had employed would continue to guide them on their path to success in the ever-evolving landscape of the IT industry in Mumbai.

6. Beyond Success: Nurturing and Retaining High-Performing Talent

In the realm of effective leadership, managing underperforming employees is a well-discussed topic. However, the art of managing high-performing individuals is equally critical and demands a unique approach. These exceptional employees consistently deliver outstanding results, setting the bar high for themselves and their colleagues. As leaders, it becomes our responsibility to not only harness their potential but also ensure their continued engagement and growth within the organization. In this article, we will explore ten strategies to effectively manage and retain high-performing employees, diving deep into each approach and offering insights into the art of keeping these exceptional talents motivated and fulfilled. By understanding the intricacies of managing high-performing individuals, we can create an environment that nurtures their skills, fosters their growth, and ultimately contributes to the long-term success of both the employees and the organization. So, let us embark on this journey of exploring the key strategies to manage and keep high-performing employees engaged, ultimately unlocking their true potential and driving exceptional results.

Here, we will explore ten strategies for successfully managing and retaining high-performing employees, providing an in-depth analysis of each point.

Recognize and Appreciate: High-performing employees thrive on recognition and appreciation. It is crucial to acknowledge their exceptional contributions and achievements regularly. By providing sincere and specific recognition, publicly celebrating their successes, and highlighting their impact, you reinforce their value and foster a sense of pride and engagement.

Offer growth and development opportunities: High-performing employees are driven by a desire for continuous learning and growth. To keep them engaged, provide challenging assignments, projects, or leadership roles that allow them to stretch their capabilities. Offer opportunities for skill development through training programs, workshops, or mentoring relationships. Engage in regular conversations about their career aspirations and create a development plan tailored to their goals.

Foster a Positive Work Environment: Creating a positive and supportive work culture is vital for retaining high-performing employees. Encourage open communication, collaboration, and idea-sharing among team members. Foster a sense of camaraderie and promote work-life balance. Ensure that the workplace is inclusive, diverse, and respectful, where every employee feels valued and appreciated.

Provide Autonomy and Trust: High-performing employees thrive when given autonomy and trust in their work. Delegate meaningful responsibilities and allow them to make decisions and take ownership of their projects. Provide guidance and support when needed, but avoid micromanaging. Trust their expertise, and give them the freedom to innovate and explore new ideas.

Set Stretch Goals: Challenging high-performing employees with stretch goals is essential for their growth and motivation. These goals should push them outside their comfort zones and provide opportunities for personal and professional development. Collaborate with them to establish clear objectives that align with their skills, interests, and the organization's strategic priorities. Regularly monitor progress, offer feedback, and adjust goals as necessary.

Encourage Collaboration and Recognition: Promote collaboration among high-performing employees and encourage them to share their knowledge and skills with others. Create opportunities for cross-functional projects or teams where they can collaborate with colleagues from different departments. Encourage peer recognition and create platforms for high performers to acknowledge and appreciate the efforts of their teammates.

Provide Competitive Compensation and Benefits: To retain high-performing employees, ensure they are fairly compensated for their exceptional contributions. Regularly review their salaries and benefits to align with industry standards and reward their performance. Consider additional incentives such as bonuses, profit-sharing, or performance-based rewards to recognize and motivate their efforts.

Seek Their Input and Feedback: Demonstrate that the opinions and ideas of high-performing employees are valued by actively seeking their input on important decisions or projects. Encourage them to provide feedback on processes, strategies, or organizational improvements. Actively listen to their suggestions and implement changes when feasible. This involvement gives them a sense of ownership and shows that their contributions are instrumental in shaping the organization.

Regularly check-in and Provide Support: Schedule regular one-on-one meetings to check-in with high-performing employees. Use these conversations to understand their needs, address any challenges they may be facing, and provide necessary support or resources. Actively listen to their aspirations, concerns, and goals, and offer guidance or mentorship where applicable. This demonstrates your commitment to their growth and well-being.

Encourage Work-Life Balance: Recognize the importance of work-life balance and promote practices that prioritize employee well-being. Encourage high-performing employees to take breaks, utilize their vacation time, and maintain a healthy work-life integration. Foster a supportive environment that respects boundaries and encourages self-care.

In the world of leadership, **managing high-performing employees is an art that requires finesse, adaptability, and a deep understanding of their unique needs.** These exceptional individuals possess extraordinary skills and consistently deliver outstanding results, propelling organizations to new heights. By implementing the strategies discussed in this article—recognizing and appreciating their contributions, offering growth opportunities, fostering a positive work environment, providing autonomy, setting stretch goals, encouraging collaboration and recognition, offering competitive compensation, seeking their input, providing support, and promoting work-life balance—

leaders can effectively manage and retain their high-performing talent.

When high-performing employees feel valued, challenged, and supported, their engagement soars, and their potential is unleashed. They become catalysts for innovation by driving positive change and inspiring their peers. By nurturing their growth, leaders not only benefit from their exceptional performance but also create a culture that attracts and retains top talent, bolstering the organization's long-term success.

Remember, managing high-performing employees is a continuous journey that requires ongoing effort and adaptation. It necessitates a deep understanding of their aspirations, fears, and motivations. By investing in their development and providing the necessary support, leaders can build lasting relationships with these exceptional individuals, fostering loyalty and creating a sense of purpose.

As we conclude our exploration of managing high-performing employees, let us embrace the responsibility to unleash their potential and keep them engaged. By doing so, we create a harmonious synergy between their aspirations and the organization's goals. Together, we can achieve remarkable outcomes, drive innovation, and shape a future where high-performing employees thrive and organizations flourish. So, let us embark on this journey, embracing the art of managing high-performing employees and witnessing the transformative power they bring to our organizations.

7. The Most Underrated Management Tool – FEEDBACK

Employee engagement is a critical contributor to business success and growth. However, organizations and HR are finding it increasingly difficult to engage employees, get them to be more productive, and perform to the best of their abilities. The Gallup State of the Global Workplace Report 2017 found that nearly 85% of employees across the globe fall into the categories of actively disengaged or not engaged. Even the best talent can feature in the actively disengaged category because the organization, manager, leader, or HR is able to make them feel valued or motivated to work. They actively or passively keep looking for newer and better jobs, and when it comes around, they move on. Organizations are at a growing risk of losing the best talent if they are not able to engage them. The inability to retain talent is detrimental in today's day and age when the war for talent is on.

Accordingly, HR and organizations are making efforts to improve employee performance and productivity through a range of employee engagement initiatives and management measures, such as higher remuneration, lavish perks, CSR initiatives, crafting positive work environments, and so on. In this scheme of things, one very potent management tool that could turn around employee engagement and help create a culture of high performance but is most underrated is feedback.

WHAT MAKES FEEDBACK SUCH A POTENT AND VALUABLE TOOL?

Feedback, by definition, is about providing information, reactions, or statements of opinion about a person's performance on a task that serves as a basis for improvement. Contrary to popular belief, it is not limited to criticism or having to be negative all the time. Negative feedback and criticism are two types of feedback that managers and leaders should consciously stay away from. There are other preferred types of feedback—positive, constructive, feedforward, praise, instructional, motivational, etc.—that must be given at the right time, in the right way, and in the right place. Put differently, feedback needs to be effective and delivered in a way that employees are able to take action based on it.

Effective feedback enables employees to improve job performance by enhancing ability, valuing effort, and recognizing results. It enables them to understand their performance from a third-person perspective, providing rich insights on strengths and weaknesses.

Reduce mistakes on the job and increase their efficiency on the job if provided consistently, clearly, and constructively. Even top performers may have certain skill gaps (soft skills or interpersonal skills), inadvertent behavior, and other deficiencies that effective feedback can help them rectify before they escalate into something bigger.

Understand the manager's, leader's, and organization's expectations from them, and accordingly, set goals and objectives for the short and long-term.

Resolve challenges that they are facing on the personal and professional front that are hindering their performance. It also enables them to remove uncertainties, gain confidence, and improve self-esteem and self-worth.

Learn faster if the feedback is continuous and constructive.

Engage in meaningful discussions and build positive workplace relationships.

Feel more valued, and it improves their morale, thereby enabling them to be more engaged at work.

THE MILLENNIAL POPULATION AND FEEDBACK CULTURE

Millennials comprise over 30% of the world population and are making up an increasing percentage of the workforce as well. It is predicted that by 2025, they will occupy over 75% of the global workforce. Millennials, having grown up in the age of the rapid and constant feedback loops created by social media, seek instant feedback at work too, as it helps them learn faster and grow in their jobs. When their need for instant and regular feedback is not met adequately, they feel disengaged at work and do not mind quickly moving on to an employer who will meet this demand.

Accordingly, several top organizations, such as Deloitte, Adobe, Google, etc., have adopted a positive and regular feedback culture in place of the 20th-century tool of annual performance reviews (APRs), which do not work well with the newer generations of employees. The numerous companies that have made this shift to a feedback culture have seen a noticeable rise in productivity, performance, and profitability and a reduction in absenteeism. This goes to show that an effective feedback culture has a high ROI.

EFFECTIVE FEEDBACK: HOW SHOULD IT BE?

Regular: As discussed earlier, once a year, APRs are passé.

Timely: It is ineffective if you provide feedback to an employee months after you notice something that needs changing. Effective feedback is proactive and as close to the event as possible.

Specific: Vague feedback is ineffective. You need to let employees know the specific context and instances based on which you are providing feedback for them to understand and use the feedback as actionable insights for the future.

Constructive: Criticism is a big 'NO NO'. Negative feedback should also be presented in a constructive way so that employees do not feel like they are attacked and are able to take corrective action, learn, and grow. Effective feedback must be appropriate and delivered in a tactful, non-threatening manner.

Dialogue: Effective feedback is always a dialogue between the employee and the leader, manager, peer, or coach providing the feedback, as it ensures both parties understand each other's viewpoints and are able to empathize with each other. It cannot be a monologue delivered by one party.

Personal: One-on-one feedback is the most effective. It fosters dialogue, mutual understanding, discussion on possible solutions, and better interpersonal relationships.

EMPLOYEE MINDSET IMPACTS THE WAY THEY PROCESS FEEDBACK

It is important for everyone in the organization, whether employers or employees, to understand that all feedback does not have the same desired result. Its impact varies depending on how, when, and by whom it is delivered and how the person receiving it processes the feedback cognitively. You may deliver feedback with the utmost respect, empathy, and care in a constructive manner, but it could still lead to deteriorating performance. This is because the employees receiving it may not be equipped to cognitively process the feedback the way it should be and the way you desire it to be perceived.

For instance, employees with a fixed mindset feel any feedback to be an attack on them. With his or her natural flight or fight instincts kicking in, they will either fight back, argue with the person giving the feedback, or not take the feedback seriously and continue the way they always work. Employees with a growth mindset, however, consider their skills and abilities to be malleable and look at feedback as a tool for learning and growth. So, *it is key that organizations and HR work with employees to help change their mindset and equip them to leverage the powerful tool that FEEDBACK is.*

Employees with personal traits such as low self-confidence and self-worth often find it difficult to process feedback. If they receive constructive feedback about things they can improve on and things they can avoid, their confidence and self-worth further dip, and their performance suffers. Similarly, employees who seek perfection in everything they do also find it difficult to receive feedback. With positive feedback, they keep nitpicking on their performance, not giving due credit to themselves, and with negative feedback, their stress levels go through the roof. It is key to work with such employees and enable them to process feedback better.

HOW DO YOU GIVE EFFECTIVE FEEDBACK?

The Key Do's and Don'ts: Base your feedback on credible information and be descriptive while providing feedback. Try to focus your feedback on behavior rather than on the employee's personality or character traits. Most importantly, avoid judgmental language or words. The place, time, content, and way of delivery are critical in ensuring that feedback is perceived properly and used as actionable insight for performance improvement, learning, and development.

Language Matters: Frame your thoughts appropriately, choose the right words, and then deliver feedback in the most tactful and non-threatening manner as possible. For instance, using the word 'but' could be counterproductive as people tense up on hearing the word and it accentuates the negative feedback over the positive feedback. It would be better if you said something along the lines of "You could do even better if..." or "better still...", etc., as these do not take away from the positive feedback.

Listen: Whether you are giving or receiving feedback, you must learn to listen to the other person's perspectives without interruptions, instead of hearing to argue or defend yourself.

Tying It Up with Action: Feedback is Effective and Productive Only If It is Tied to Goal-setting, an Action Plan, and Some Review Parameters; Otherwise, It Would Be a Waste of Work Hours.

EMBED FEEDBACK IN YOUR WORKPLACE CULTURE

Giving and receiving feedback on a regular basis must become a key part of your organizational culture. This will ensure that every employee, leader, and manager understands that feedback is the basis for professional and organizational development and that they should not shy away from seeking and providing feedback to their peers, managers, and teams. Start with your leadership to ensure buy-in. HR and organizations must take measures to embed feedback in their workplace culture and make it an integral part of the job experience for everyone.

8A. Developing High-Performing Teams in the Post-Pandemic Era

TRUST – THE MOST CRITICAL ELEMENT OF TEAM DYNAMICS

"Teamwork is the ability to work together toward a common vision. The ability to direct individual accomplishments toward organizational objectives. It is the fuel that allows common people to attain uncommon results."

– Andrew Carnegie

INTRODUCTION

Team dynamics are the unconscious, psychological forces that influence the direction of a team's behavior and performance. They are like undercurrents in the sea, which can carry boats in a different direction from the one they intend to sail.

Team dynamics are created by the nature of the team's work, the personalities within the team, their working relationships with other people, and the environment in which the team works.

Kurt Lewin, a social psychologist, and change management expert is credited with coining the term "group or Team Dynamics" in early 1939. He noted that people often take on distinct roles and behaviors when they work in a group. "Group dynamics" describes the effects of these roles and behaviors on other group members, and on the group as a whole.

A team with a positive dynamic is easy to spot. Team members trust one another, they work towards a collective decision, and they hold one another accountable for making things happen. As well as this, researchers have found that when a team has a positive dynamic, its members are nearly twice as creative as an average group. Team dynamics can be good - for example, when they improve overall team performance and/or get the best out of individual team members.

In a group with poor group dynamics, people's behavior disrupts work. As a result, the group may not come to any decision, or it may make the wrong choice because group members could not explore options effectively. Examples of bad team dynamics are when they cause unproductive conflict and demotivation, and prevent the team from achieving its goals.

Characteristics of Team Dynamics that Make for a Winning Team -

1. **Shared Purpose**
2. **Trust and Openness**
3. **Willingness to Correct Mistakes**
4. **Diversity and Inclusion**
5. **Interdependence and a Sense of Belonging**

6. **Consensus Decision Making**

7. **Participative Leadership**

As they rightly say, **"The difference between success and failure is a great team".**

THE PANDEMIC YEAR –

Because of the global pandemic, many of us are now working from home so that we can maintain social distancing. The pandemic has also caused massive disruption. We have dealt with loved ones getting sick and dying. Kids have had to do school over video from their kitchens while parents, who have full-time jobs, are supposed to supervise.

Then there is the uncertainty. We do not know when, or if, anything is going back to normal or what the world on the other side of this will be like.

But those hard facts put down on paper do not tell the whole story, and that is because the less tangible, more human consequences of remote working are easily overlooked. Businesses are made up of people after all, and how those people feel and interact with each other is a vital part of how businesses operate smoothly and can grow. The pandemic year has changed the rules of the game forever. It has changed the way we will be working in 2021 and beyond. It has changed TEAM DYNAMICS.

In this new world, the whats of leadership haven't changed, but some of the hows have, and it is those small differences that can make a big difference in three dimensions - **for you, for your team members, and your organization.** The bottom line is this - **You need to think leadership first, location second.**

TRUST – THE MOST CRITICAL ELEMENT OF TEAM DYNAMICS

Can I trust you? Can you trust me? What does it even mean to trust someone?

As John Pepper, the former CEO of P&G once said, "Despite its powerful benefit, trust is the single "hardest quality to create in any organization, "and it's fragile."

When we talk about a trusting team or trusting partners, I think very often we forget that trust is not an instruction, trust is a feeling. You cannot tell someone to trust you. No leader can just tell their company, "Trust me." It does not work that way. Trust is a feeling. It is a biological, feeling that comes from the environment we are in.

Trust inherently means risk, so why take that risk? Why not do the project yourself so you are not counting on anyone else? Well because the big ambitions in life require collaboration. We cannot do it all alone.

Trustworthiness in a team set-up is evaluated on two primary criteria - **Competency and warmth.** Competency is how others decide if you have what it takes. The expertise, and the reliability to come through for them. Warmth is how they decide your willingness to come through. Are you a friend or foe? Will you prioritize your interests and needs over theirs?

If someone seems warm, seems friendly, but does not have a clue what he is doing, we would be unlikely to trust him with any responsibility. We might like him or pity him, but we will not trust him. If someone has high competency but lacks warmth, we might respect or envy him, we might think wow, he knows a ton, but I am not sure he has my best interests at heart, so I'm not sure I trust him.

If someone lacks warmth and competency, we feel disdain and certainly no trust.

And the quadrant we want to be in is high competency and high warmth because this is where trust happens.

Even when someone has both warmth and competency, **trust is situational.**

So now that you have a better understanding of the nature of trust, be patient with people who are slow to trust you even though you are a genuinely trustworthy person.

They have no guarantee of your future behavior, and they are taking a risk on you.

On those trust dimensions warmth and competency. Learning to trust and to be worthy of trust is one of life's most challenging and rewarding tasks.

Building Trust in Virtual Teams: When we work with colleagues globally, trust is essential. Without trust, we slow down collaboration and the achievement of results and incur a tax on trust in checking and monitoring activity. However, at the same time, trust is harder to build when we rarely get face-to-face, and we may experience cultural differences or misunderstandings due to communicating through technology. In the past, trust-building was a free by-product of being in the same location. We had time to get to know each other over coffee or lunch or socializing in the evening. Today, when we have limited face-to-face time, we need to be more intentional about building trust.

As discussed previously, in the early stages of building trust, we typically pay attention to two types of signals. The first is competency. Does the person have the ability to do the job, and do they respond reliably and accurately to our requests? The second is warmth. Do they respond in a way that shows that they wish to collaborate and that they share our values?

In working together remotely, competence is not so hard to evaluate. If you are trying to build trust quickly, concentrate on responding fast, giving a good quality answer, and offering more help. If you are trying to help a colleague build trust quickly, make sure they can deliver quick wins and tell your colleagues when they do so.

Evaluating warmth, however, can be much more difficult remotely, under cross-cultural barriers. The main signals may only be coming through email. If we can get face-to-face, this accelerates trust-building. If we cannot, then we should look to create opportunities for people to work together via video and to get to know each other as quickly as possible.

As we receive confirmation of the competency and warmth of our colleagues, we take successive steps to higher levels of trust. We also call this the staircase of trust.

If you are leading a global team, think about the ways you can enable team members to demonstrate both their competence and their warmth to their colleagues. If you do not, then trust will develop anyway, but it will take longer to happen, and you may have misunderstandings along the way. So, remember to keep trust in your global leadership agenda and to create the conditions for trust to form quickly.

Here are a few strategies that can help you build trust, in a virtual context -

Socialize in virtual meetings: People get to know and trust one another through small talk. We lack hallways and water coolers on virtual teams. So, make time for socializing.

Be a connector: Help others on the team get to know one another. Unmute during meetings, unless your background is noisy. Some background noise, like a crying baby, humanizes us. And conversation and laughter are more spontaneous when we are unmuted.

Clarify roles and expectations: In shared space teams we see and hear what others are working on. So, we know if there's an overlap in our work. In virtual teams, we must work harder to clarify expectations.

Rotate power: Virtual teams with high degrees of trust, shift power among the members, depending on who has the most knowledge, for each stage of work.

Share the time zone burden: No one person should always have to get up for the 3 AM call.

And finally, **be reliable** - In virtual settings, reliability is the strongest predictor of trust. Make sure you are on time for meetings and follow through on what you say you will do. Virtually, your word is all you have.

8B. Developing High-Performing Teams in the Post-Pandemic Era

EFFECTIVE COMMUNICATION – FUEL THAT DRIVES TEAM DYNAMICS

In the past few years, collaboration was listed as one of the top five skills employers need the most. Your ability to work well with others on a team is essential for developing your career in just about every field, from health care to government, sports, education, tech, and the military. We find ourselves working in teams, why?

Research shows that effective teams produce better outcomes than individuals or uncoordinated groups. And yet, many teams struggle to reach their potential. Or to put it another way, as Malcolm Gladwell has said, "The kinds of errors that cause plane crashes are invariably errors of teamwork and communication."

Whether you're a newly minted team or you've been working together for years, there's likely room for improvement in the ways you communicate and collaborate. By giving everyone on the team defined roles and responsibilities, you can better coordinate and avoid duplicate efforts and missed opportunities.

Some key collaboration process roles to consider are the meeting convener, recorder, and monitor. Depending on the nature of your team, each of these roles can be subdivided into more specific roles for your team, and these don't necessarily need to be aligned with your functional roles in the organization. Think of these as separate working titles for your specific team.

The convener is a role the team leader often takes at least partially, especially if he or she is accountable for the outcome of the team's efforts. Convening includes everything from determining whether or not a meeting is needed, to ensuring the agenda is developed and shared, to scheduling the actual meeting time and place.

The recorder is responsible for keeping detailed notes on the discussion that takes place during the meeting. Notes should include a list of the participants, a summary of the discussion associated with each agenda item, and a list of the next steps. Any follow-up items should have names associated with them so that it's clear who will be acting on whatever next steps you've discussed. Shortly after each meeting, this person should send a copy of the minutes to the team and allow participants to clarify or add to the document as needed. The action items from the minutes are often a topic for the agenda of the next team meeting.

A monitor will help the group stick to the agenda items and keep the discussion within the time allotted. Keeping groups focused, particularly if you're meeting virtually, can be extremely challenging. It's really easy to get off-topic. This person should feel comfortable interrupting the discussion if it goes off in a tangential direction. When this happens, the monitor may ask the recorder to note that this topic needs to be an agenda item for a future meeting.

Some teams divide out these roles and keep them the same for every meeting. Others swap roles regularly to make sure this important labor is evenly distributed throughout the team.

However, you choose to assign responsibilities, having defined roles will help you keep your team meetings focused and meaningful. If your team is operating without assigned process roles, add this to your next meeting agenda.

As a team, it's important to be in alignment with your goals, purpose, and process for collaborating. Otherwise, you're like a group of rowers on a boat rowing in different directions and different paces.

You'll want to spend some time discussing your purpose. Why has your team been convened? What is it about this specific group of people and the unique task at hand, that you as a group have been trusted to address? And how will you do it?

When it comes to setting goals, choose a template that makes sense for your team, whether it's KPIs, SMART, or SMARTER goals, or some other performance metric.

Make sure your team collectively establishes shared goals for your work together. Once you've established your goals, take a few minutes to discuss your conditions of satisfaction. These are the minimal requirements to reach completion of a project.

Conditions of satisfaction are different than goals. If your team's goals are on the high end of what you hope to accomplish as a group, the conditions of satisfaction are on the low end. What's the bare minimum everyone will be comfortable with having completed? For example, for students, the goal in a course might be to earn an A on an assignment, but the condition of satisfaction would be a passing grade.

Teams often set lofty goals initially but adjust their expectations once the work requirements are understood. Having a clear definition of what is acceptable before you start your project, will save you time, and frustration down the line.

With your goals and conditions of satisfaction in mind, you'll want to develop a team charter. A document that outlines commitments for how your team will collaborate on your work together.

This document should spell out all of your expectations around the process, for how you'll work together to accomplish your goals.

Typical team charters include ground rules for team meetings, norms for communicating with each other, details for how you'll make decisions, consequences for not meeting expectations, and what you'll do if you experience conflict.

The idea is to spell out the ways you plan to work with each other, to help avoid misunderstandings, or clashes in working styles.

Assigning roles for communicating in team meetings and establishing conditions of satisfaction will help get your team in sync, and make sure you're all rowing in the same direction.

Reasonable people with the same goals will approach projects differently. This is why teams must document expectations and norms for how they'll work together.

The team's charter should establish some ground rules for how to handle these types of things. After your team has decided on norms for communication, operating procedures, and general expectations, you can document all of this in your team charter.

Cross-cultural communication within teams: It's well established that today's teams are global and teams that harness their diverse perspectives and talents have better outcomes than those who don't. And yet, communicating across cultures can present some challenges.

A model to help you think through the cultural issues that can come up in cross-cultural business communication is abbreviated as **LESCANT**. This points to seven areas - **language, environment social organization, context, authority, nonverbal, and time.**

To consider international business settings, I'll briefly highlight some things to consider in each of the seven areas, starting with L, language.

When it comes to your language, use clear and basic phrasing whenever possible. While everyone on your team may be using the same language, it's easy for information to get lost in translation. The same words can have different meanings in different parts of the same country. Keep in mind, that everyone on your team may not have the same level of language fluency, and that may influence how they participate in group discussions, especially if things unexpectedly come up. It's easy to confuse language proficiency with confidence, but that can be a mistake. A teammate may have strong evidence to support an idea and have some trouble articulating it, or vice versa.

In terms of E, environment, what external cultural factors impact your team's work or dynamics? This can include aspects of your physical realities and a host of other external factors. Next, how are the cultures represented on your team socially organized? How do religion, race, gender, and class factor into the societies your team is constructed of? One example that can be tied to friction in teams is how people view individualism versus collectivism.

The next letter, C, is context. Which of your teammates are from high- or low-context cultures? In a high-context culture, communication is explicit. Communicators are direct and verbalize every word they need to get their point across. In a low-context culture, communication is implicit and relies more on non-verbal cues, silence, and the unsaid. Recognizing these subtle differences will improve your team's communication.

The next consideration, A, is authority. How do your teammates view authority? Our perspectives on authority, power, and leadership style are all informed by our cultural background and personal preferences. If there are hierarchies based on title or age within your team, keep in mind that may prevent some teammates from pushing back on an idea from a more senior teammate.

Our N, nonverbal communication, speaks volumes. Within your team, pay attention to the unsaid things. If you notice from their body language that a teammate seems to withdraw or might want to speak, but can't get into the conversation, you can be an ally for that person by creating an opening for them. If you don't want to put them on the spot, follow up individually and find out how your teammate wants you to act in the future. Remember, the best ideas don't necessarily come from the chattiest people.

And finally, T is time, which I'd argue is our most valuable resource. How individuals perceive time, and their schedules varies. Some teammates may see time as more fluid or flexible, whereas others follow a more exact and literal timing.

The LESCANT model gives us seven considerations for communicating in our cross-cultural teams. If you don't know what your teammates think about each of these categories, plan to have a discussion about these topics and link them to your team charter. Your team is only as strong as your ability to effectively communicate across cultural boundaries.

Manage conflict within teams: Not all conflict is bad. Conflict in teams is inevitable. And if you manage it productively, it can lead to positive outcomes in your work. But, if conflict on your team is mismanaged, a seemingly small misunderstanding can quickly spiral out of control.

There are lots of reasons that reasonable people working together towards the same goals, may experience different types of team conflict. Avoiding or ignoring it, won't make them go away. There are two sources of conflict teams often face that I want to differentiate, **task** and **interpersonal.** Let›s talk a bit about each.

Task conflict is tied to disagreements about how your work gets done. This can be about what constitutes the actual deliverable, or about the process for getting to the deliverable. Diverse teams have more potential for task conflict because teammates are addressing problem-solving from different perspectives.

Whether they're drawing from their personal experience or disciplinary expertise, they see the work differently and have different ideas about how to address it. Some of these differences are interpersonal differences, such as values, personality, needs, and preferences.

Oftentimes, there isn't necessarily a right or wrong on these topics. It's simply that people view or have experienced these issues differently. As a result, teammates must find a way to agree to disagree and learn from each other's perspective.

When you notice conflict happening on your team, the first step is to identify which type of conflict you're dealing with. Both types of conflict are tied to miscommunication, so we can use effective communication strategies to mitigate and resolve conflict in our teams.

The first step is to acknowledge the conflict. Awkward tension will just fester and make things uncomfortable for everyone. The first step is to identify that there is a problem. Now, we're on our way to resolving it.

Second, identify a good time for a discussion. Whether this conversation includes the entire team or just those involved with the conflict is up to you all. But find a good time to meet in a neutral space. It's important to have ground rules for how you'll conduct these conversations. If you think emotions are too raw, consider bringing in a neutral third party to moderate and facilitate the discussion.

Third, give each person equal time to articulate their perspective. The key here is to understand the perspective of your teammate. Notice I said understand and not agree with. After everyone has had a chance to share their perspective, each teammate has the choice to determine how they want to proceed. Some teams like to end the conversation there and take time to think about what they've learned. Others choose to continue the discussion. Based on the information that's been shared, you may want to apologize for something you said or did. Or you can simply thank the person for sharing their perspective.

Fourth and finally, as a team, consider how this can be avoided in the future. What can you learn about what's happened here, and how can you grow to improve for the future? Many misunderstandings or miscommunications occur as a result of not thoughtfully developing a team charter.

With strong inter-team communication, you can reduce conflict and leverage it for your team's benefit.

Communicating virtually within teams: Virtual teams experience some unique benefits and challenges. Luckily, there are things we can do to improve the performance of virtual teams by focusing on our team's communication.

One of the most important things you can do is take the extra time to build connections with your colleagues. This might not feel natural at first, but it's critical, relationships matter.

Three ways you can get to know your teammates virtually are - one, create virtual spaces or times for conversations. Open office hours or town hall-style meetings give people a chance to check in and voice ideas or concerns.

Two, post monthly or quarterly virtual socials. A happy hour, trivia, or game night is a fun way to connect with your team outside of your work.

Three, ask good questions. If I ask you how you're doing, you'll likely respond with a one-word answer.

It's become somewhat of an ignored greeting to ask someone how they're doing and for them to respond with good or okay. To get people to open up, ask open-ended questions. For example, tell me about how your day is going or what's new in your world. This opens the door for the person to talk about themselves, a spouse, child, pet, or whatever they want to share.

Building relationships is just as important for virtual teams. So, it's important to make an effort here. When it comes to work-related communication, there are tons of tools you can use to share information within your team.

You want to use the right technology for the task and keep things as simple as possible. And keep in mind how the recipient of the information is likely to respond. Emails are great for informational updates and chat is useful for real-time information but remember to pick up the phone or turn on the video camera and have a live discussion when you need to talk about delicate or sensitive matters.

Document everything using an agreed-upon method that is easily accessible to everyone on the team. This may seem like overkill, but over-communication keeps everyone informed. Chances are, your team uses chat, email, phone, video conferencing, text messaging, and so on.

Pick one central place to regularly update and store information so that everyone is aware of work status and next steps. You don't want to have to go back and check five or six different communication platforms to find information when you need it.

Even if your team is dispersed across the globe, you can take comfort in knowing you're operating at an optimal level when you invest in good team communication.

New signals and devices: We all know the importance of nonverbal communication to interpret meaning. When someone is talking, you take note of their body language, tone of voice, facial expressions, and eye contact. So, while it is impractical to assume every workplace interaction will be in person, it is critical to learn how to assess the new signals of digital body language to find better ways to connect with our colleagues.

So, what digital body language signals are you sending in your messages?

I am talking about signals like your word choice; the response time to a message; your email signature; who you cc: forward, bcc: on your emails; the order of the email recipients on an email; switching from one medium to another; the use of punctuation, abbreviations, emojis; and many more.

First, we have to try to consider how our digital body language signals may be received by others.

For instance, Mohsin, a manager I coach, told me about an interaction with his boss that left him feeling underappreciated. He had sent her a detailed plan about a business issue with a top customer. Mohsin, had stayed up all night working on it, and when he sent this detailed brief with a list of questions, he asked her to answer by the next day.

He expected her to respond quickly and maybe with a few follow-up questions that Mohsin could explore. Instead, he waited until 4:00 p.m. the following day and all he heard back was K, period. That is all.

Mohsin was confused and a little insulted. First, he felt his clear and comprehensive proposal deserved a proper response. Was his leader considering the issue? Mohsin could not tell by her response. Second, did K mean he should proceed or that he should put the idea on the back burner? Again, he could not tell.

And finally, he thought that she could offer a response amounting to more than a single letter.

This is just a simple example of the importance of the new signals in digital body language.

Now, there is no perfect etiquette for digital body language, but what I want to do is share with you three questions you should ask yourself that will provide you with a way to understand and use digital body language signals more effectively.

The first question - Did I give the other person enough context in my message? Is it clear by my digital body language signals? Context requires us to use those signals carefully.

The second question - Am I using the right emotional tone in my digital body language? Am I trying to show gratitude, respect, alignment, or frustration in my communications? How could I use new signals, like periods, question marks, and exclamations, to show emotion in the right ways?

And last question, am I showing a clear call to action or a next step? Does the recipient know if this is an opinion or an action request? And is it clear what to do next? With all the new signals we have, when sending even the briefest of messages, remember to carefully read and write any communication you send or receive.

Here are some other tips for hosting more effective virtual meetings:

- Use collaborative meeting software like WebEx, GoToMeeting, or Adobe Connect, which allows you to see others on your team. These programs also allow you to use a hand icon to manage the conversation.

- Telepresence technology takes this a step further, with more sophisticated programs to make you feel like you're meeting in person. These programs include Cisco's Telepresence series and Polycom high-definition conferencing.

- Keep in mind that employees who work from home aren't always ready for a video call. Remember to ask first before calling them on video.

- Host meetings only when necessary; avoid status-update meetings.

- Assign agenda items to various people on your team to keep them engaged during the meeting.

- Maintain team involvement throughout the session; use polls or collect votes.

- Limit meeting times to stay on track.

- Appoint someone to keep the conversation on track when the conversation turns to tangents.

- Direct individual questions or unrelated discussions offline so you're not wasting time during meetings.

- Share the agenda and any notes on your screen so that the whole team can see them.

- Consider recording meetings and reposting the recordings.

8C. Developing High-Performing Teams in the Post-Pandemic Era

LEADING FROM THE FRONT

As a result of COVID-19, many of us have stepped into a new reality of virtual working, which poses new challenges for leaders. That virtual is not physical, and team connection and productivity will not automatically continue in a virtual world. Virtual teaming affords many benefits but presents a higher risk of misalignment and lack of collaboration, which may take a toll on team trust and employee engagement if not done right.

Distance and lack of face-to-face communication make managing virtual teams a challenge. When people are not in the same location, it can be hard to understand what they are saying. It is easy to misinterpret their meaning. And unless you can video conference, you do not get the benefit of reading body language or facial expressions. That is why you need excellent communication to manage virtual teams.

It's tough but not impossible to build long-distance relationships. The same interpersonal skills you use with office mates work with remote team members, too.

Be clear in your communication, confirm understanding, be supportive and respectful, take care of your people and help them overcome obstacles, and do not forget to thank them and tell them when they do good work.

Misunderstandings, communication issues, and cultural differences, all can create conflict. It is never easy to resolve conflict. It is even more challenging with virtual teams. Email is too impersonal for delicate discussions. Plus, it can lead to even more misunderstanding.

Instead, use phone or video conferencing to work through conflict. Speaking of phone and video conferencing, figuring out when to hold a group session can be tough. Someone is usually up late or much too early. Once you sort out the best time for calls, hold an initial session to talk about how communication will work on the team.

Understanding the manager's connecting role in a remote team: Now to me, the main purpose of the manager is the care and feeling of the team members, making sure that they have everything they need to complete their jobs. The manager may roll up their sleeves at times to pitch in, but that's not their primary purpose. Rather, they have the responsibility for monitoring overall team performance, schedule and workload and making sure everything comes together as planned. In addition to these tasks, the manager of a remote team has some special responsibilities.

Primarily, I think the remote manager needs to act as the hub that connects the geographically disconnected team. They're the ones who are going to be the primary contact back at the command center and would like to be the pass-through point for information flowing to the remote workers from corporate. This isn't to say,

"I don't think there should not be direct communication with the remote employees from the company". There absolutely should be if the company wants to keep the workers engaged and informed, but the manager holds a pivotal role for the team as the intermediary for a lot of activities. This is going to require some special effort.

Setting Ground Rules: Make sure that there are well-documented procedures in place and that they are being consistently followed. How can a team have a solid basis for performance if the requirements of that performance have not been defined?

This is important for any team, but I think it's even more critical for remote groups.

Since the individuals on the team may not interact with each other as frequently as a co-located team, there is a lot more opportunity for them to head off in different directions unless there is a solid understanding upfront.

For me, this is one of the manager's most important jobs. It is ultimately the manager's responsibility to make sure everyone on the team understands their role. Making sure there are adequate definitions of the work at hand and that individual tasks and deliverables are spelled out provides team members with actionable goals to meet, reduces ambiguity, and sets common ground. All of these will contribute to an increase in group trust, and by the way, consistency and application are really important here.

You as the manager must apply rules around procedures and performance to everyone on the team equally.

It's much better to set the expectations and have rules in place upfront and have everyone follow them consistently. Building a level playing field makes it fair for the whole team.

Developing working agreements and defined norms in a virtual team: Just because it's the manager's responsibility to make sure procedures and expectations are in place doesn't mean that they are the only ones developing them. Managers must get the input of the team whenever they are standardizing processes or setting goals.

First of all, your team members are the experts at what it takes to get the job done. They're the ones who know what steps need to be taken, and in what order. And they're the ones who know where the process can get bogged down. Maybe there's a spot where work has to pass through a gate that's controlled by someone outside the team. Maybe there's a manual process that ought to be automated. Or information required that isn't provided through standard input forms that team members have to then go and research. Whatever the case, involving the team in setting up the process means everyone is invested in it and its success. I also think that creating a team working agreement is extremely valuable.

How do the team members want to communicate? When will people be available? What are mutually agreeable service levels and turnaround times? Who is available to help with specific tasks?

Giving people a good understanding of how the team operates means they'll be able to integrate that much quicker. While this is a good idea for any team, I think it's especially important for remote teams to have a solidly defined set of norms. It will smooth team interactions, build trust among team members, and bake in accountability.

All important factors to overall team health and success. But at the end of the day, it's the manager's job to guide the team in this process of creation. And it's their responsibility to make sure everything that the team will need is in place.

Setting Accountability in a Virtual Setup: Virtual employees need to take more individual responsibility to meet deadlines, so someone must hold them accountable even though virtual managers have fewer opportunities to observe their employees. To address this dilemma, project management software is an effective tool. Software programs such as Basecamp, WorkZone, and Wrike can make each project visible to the entire team so that everyone concerned understands where their job fits into the big picture. The ability to share files, assign tasks, and check due dates also allows team members to easily communicate the next steps, whether it's providing data or passing along a document for review.

Time-tracking software (such as TimeFox, Timesheet, and Kronos) is also an effective tool for improving virtual team performance, allowing team leaders to track hours (especially helpful if you work with multiple clients and you're trying to determine how much time you're investing in each one).

Other habits that help leaders manage accountability and improve decision-making in a virtual environment include:

- Develop metrics that focus on results, not the number of hours worked.

- Involve employees in the early project planning stages so realistic deadlines can be developed.

- Give employees more autonomy by allowing them to determine the best way to organize their work.

- Schedule check-ins at key milestones with individual team members to assess progress, provide feedback and coaching, and make required course corrections.

- Share calendars and action plans with the entire team so that everyone is aware of the status of a project.

Keeping track of what your virtual team members are doing: With so many working remotely today, leaders are now facing a set of challenges that didn't exist before. How do you keep track of what everyone on your team is doing when they are potentially thousands of miles apart? Here are four strategies you might find helpful.

First, set clear goals and expectations. Openly discuss performance metrics, deadlines, and delivery milestones. You'll also want to establish a defined system to monitor their progress, either with a shared dashboard or regular status check-ins.

The key is to hold each team member accountable for their deliverables without micromanaging.

Second, emphasize ongoing communication. Create a pattern of consistent interaction with your team as a group and one-on-one.

Be explicit about your preferred guidelines for team communication, what types of messages they should share with you and with others and how often they should provide those.

When you set a good example for effective communication, your team members will likely follow your lead.

Third, leverage technology to keep your team connected. To integrate the work of your virtual team members, you'll need to find the tools, software, or apps that meet your specific needs.

You can find options like Slack that enable anytime, anywhere chatting.

A system like Basecamp can help to keep your team informed about progress and changes in real-time.

Platforms like Doodle can dramatically increase the efficiency of scheduling for a virtual group.

You might also consider using collaborative tools like Google Docs or Microsoft Flow.

These allow for real-time collaboration and support anytime and anywhere-access to a multitude of documents.

And just because your team is scattered doesn't mean you can't have daily huddles. It's important to schedule regular meetings through video conferencing like Skype or Zoom.

These virtual gatherings will help to build a sense of community and reinforce the importance of working collaboratively when proximity isn't an option.

Fourth, ask for feedback and provide ongoing support. When you aren't physically working in an office down the hall, you lose some opportunities to detect problems that may be brewing. So, in a virtual team setting, you must get candid feedback regularly.

Ask your staff members what they need from you to be more successful. What challenges are they facing?

You could gather that information in a one-on-one video chat or maybe through a virtual suggestion box. And then here is the main message. Respond, take action, and make sure your team members know you're listening and are willing to provide the support they need.

When you apply these strategies, you can transform a diverse set of remote workers into a dynamic, collaborative team with the potential to achieve impressive results.

Virtually Motivating Your Employees: Virtual team members face frequent distractions and many unique challenges that can affect their motivation, especially if they work from home. Virtual workers often feel isolated and as a result, can lose sight of why their contributions matter.

Here are some practical ways to keep your virtual team motivated:

- Practice active listening: paraphrase what your employees say to confirm understanding since there are more opportunities for misunderstandings without visual cues.
- Don't assume that your instructions are clear; have team members summarize the assigned task before taking it on
- Make yourself available outside normal business hours.
- Minimize the use of email; encourage team members to schedule conversations with each other as they collaborate on a project.
- Instant messaging tools like Google Hangouts, Google Talk, Microsoft Lync (now Skype for Business), and Cisco Jabber allow you to check in with team members in a less formal way.
- Make it easy for all employees to access the documents they need remotely. Using cloud-based file-sharing software, such as Google Drive or Dropbox, can help everyone easily share documents and stay organized.

Providing constructive feedback through virtual coaching sessions is another important way to keep team members motivated. We asked the virtual leaders we surveyed to share their best practices for coaching virtual employees. Here's what they recommended:

- Use video conferencing so you can talk face-to-face.
- Name behaviours rather than labeling. Don't tell someone her lack of commitment caused the project to fail; you're

not making it clear what she did wrong. Point to specific behaviours instead, like a failure to meet an agreed-upon deadline.

- Make the session consultative. Ask employees about their challenges and what you can do to address them together.

- Pay attention to the tone and inflection of your voice.

- Ask employees to repeat what you've said to confirm understanding.

- Don't assume they'll remember the follow-up actions; put them in writing via email.

Performance reviews in 2020 and beyond: I was having a conversation with one of my clients, the CEO of a media company. We were talking about 2020, this crazy, awful, no-good year.

He said to me, "My people don't want to do "performance appraisals this year because nobody "had a good performance."

I got a little triggered, I have to admit cause here's the thing, it's even more important to hold performance appraisals this year.

Everyone's dealing with uncertainty, but they still have a job to do.

So, let's talk about it. People are in different emotional states. Some people took advantage of remote work and ran off to Maui.

They're living their best life and if so, God bless. But some of your people moved in with their parents or are supervising kids in Zoom school or they've dealt with their health issues or family health issues and maybe problems with stress and anxiety.

So, you're going to have to deal with all of this by video.

Your job as a manager is first of all, to care, to acknowledge all the issues, create a safe space, and give them a moment to pause and process what happened this year, and then to get this year behind you and look to the future with some hope.

Even though there is a crisis, people still want to know where they stand and you might need to make sure people know what they need to do to improve and advance their careers, even in a pandemic.

So, I want to be more specific about your environment right now. Everything we've talked about still stands.

Communicate the process, even if that means at this point communicating that the process will take place next week.

Get your video set up in good shape. Schedule the time, making sure you have a buffer.

Get input from others. Use examples. Have your folks do a self-appraisal—all of it.

And then think about each employee and their circumstances. Decide what you want to communicate and how you can best make this a meaningful conversation about their performance.

Lead the appraisal conversation with compassion. Remember that through video you have to be more deliberate in showing your intent by having a sympathetic look on your face, open body language, and a softer tone of voice.

Start by acknowledging the challenges of the year and ask them to share how they experienced them.

Listen while looking directly into the camera to make eye contact over a video.

You can also open up a little bit and share some vulnerability about how it's affected you. That will help set the tone.

Then turn to the appraisal itself. You can say, "Well, I'm glad we're getting the time, "to reflect together. And I'm glad we're doing this performance review.

"I think it'll be helpful to review the year together, look at your career development goals, and build a strategy "for next year. "That's my intention today. "Let me start by sharing some of the key themes, «I noticed this year. «Then I›d like to hear what resonates with you.»

Boom, you're in.

You can and should be flexible on the goals and what was accomplished if that's called for.

You should give them a lot of time to share their thoughts and give them the benefit of the doubt.

Now, it's possible that some of your employees didn't achieve their goals that they could have or need to make some improvements.

If that's the case, start with a coaching mindset as always.

Focus on strengths and what was accomplished.

Then you can say, "Let's talk about these milestones" that you missed.

"I'd like to explore how you can improve "your time management and how you can communicate "to me earlier so there are no surprises."

Frame it as support, listen to what your employee has to say, and ask questions.

And with a game plan for next year.

Even though this year has been chaotic, your people will appreciate a performance appraisal conversation that takes into account real life and also helps them assess what they've done and plan for the future.

Get the setting right for a good virtual discussion: When you're getting ready to deliver the actual performance appraisal, you'll plan out what to say.

Considering that you'll need to do this review virtually, you need to spend just as much time planning out your setup.

Here's the thing. It's a high-stakes conversation.

You might be keyed up about it and they almost certainly are. So, let's get the basics right.

Video on, check.

Camera at eye-level, check.

A quiet, well-lit space in a place that will be free from cats running behind you and kids jumping into your lap.

So, far so good.

Now, this may sound super basic, but make sure that you're professionally dressed, and you look more or less like you would if you were in an office.

If you're working from home and balancing a lot, yourself, it's tempting to just throw on a sweatshirt.

Remember, this is a professional discussion, and you want to show your employees that you put care into it.

That starts with your appearance. So no, you don't have to put on a tie, but yes, you have to brush your hair. Put some thought into your body language.

Some people are naturally expressionless. If that's you, please alter that, and make sure you have a pleasant and inviting look on your face.

If you're unsure what that means, practice with a friend, and ask them to help you get that right. It's important when people only have video to go on.

Shift between looking directly into the camera to have eye contact and looking at them to see how they're doing.

Use open body language. If you're cold, get a sweater. Don't cross your arms. You're going to want to try to interpret their feelings as best you can.

And that takes some patience.

So, schedule an hour or more, and make sure you have a buffer before your next meeting.

Don't just do this on a call as you're driving.

One of my clients did this once. You know who you are. And don't try to squeeze it in before you have to get to a parent-teacher conference.

When you're ready to start the conversation, it's worth saying to folks, "Hey, can we both turn off all our alerts in Slack and texts?

I know it's hard to stay focused, but it's important. "If they don't want to do this discussion over video, or for some reason, they don't have great internet bandwidth, you may have to use the phone.

When you do that, try to check in at regular times during the discussion by saying,

"How is this landing with you?" Or, "Do you have any more to say about this?"

Listen to their voices. And if you hear them getting upset, stop and check-in. And over video, and even the phone, there can be a bit of a delay.

Sometimes you need to give them time to process what you're saying. Get comfortable with silence. Your virtual setup and etiquette should do everything to make them feel comfortable.

Put yourself in their shoes and pay attention to your setup, so they know that you're taking it seriously.

Measure success within teams: Right now, you might be struggling to complete a project or maybe you're ahead of schedule and under budget. If you don't know exactly why that's happening, how can you fix a problem or replicate the success?

Measuring and reflecting on your team's progress is critical for long-term success. Plan to evaluate your efforts at targeted points on your timeline when major deliverables are completed especially at the end of a project.

This doesn't have to be formal or a lengthy process. As a consultant, I do a version of this regularly. Rather than wait until the end of the project to get feedback, I typically survey my own monthly and quarterly evaluations.

If I need to pivot or make adjustments to the pace of the project, I can do so in real-time. Your team can monitor and measure your progress by conducting an after-action review.

The process is simple, and when done well, it's extremely powerful. Start by setting aside a team meeting for this discussion. Let everyone know the purpose of the meeting so they can come prepared for the discussion.

There are a few critical ground rules for effective After-Action-Reviews (AAR) that everyone needs to agree on, and leaders should make an extra effort to model.

One, **get everyone involved**. Everyone who is contributing should have an opportunity to reflect and contribute to the discussion. This conversation isn't productive if everyone, from the most junior person to the most senior executive, doesn't have a seat at the table. To that point, if you have varying levels of seniority in the room, you may need to find ways to, number two, **encourage honest discussion**. There may be cultural personality or rank-related reasons people on the team don't feel comfortable speaking up.

This brings me to number three, **dismantle hierarchies and ignore rank**. The people who are on the ground doing the work may have invaluable insights on how aspects of the project are getting done. Without making them comfortable speaking up, you risk missing out on important information that can change your work outcomes.

And finally, number four, **establish a positive environment**. This isn't the time for blaming or shaming people on the team. It's okay to speak about what did or didn't happen as planned, but the tone of the conversation must remain productive.

Now that you've established the ground rules, here are the questions for your AAR. If you have a really large group or are conducting this meeting virtually, break your team into smaller groups so that everyone is engaged in the discussion and then reconvene after everyone's had a chance to share their ideas.

Number one, **what was supposed to happen**? This seems like an obvious question. If everyone isn't in alignment on this question, you want to revisit the team's goals and expectations next time.

Two, **what did happen?** Did we meet our goal and only our goal? Or, were there unexpected outcomes, either positive or negative, that also came along with accomplishing our goal?

Three, **what worked well and why?** What did we do a good job with and why did it work so well? It›s important to understand why we›ve been so successful.

Fourth, **what do we need to change and why?** It›s also important to know what didn›t go as planned and have a good understanding of why things got derailed.

Five, **how can we improve our process going forward?** A thoughtful discussion about what we can do better in the future gives your team a revised roadmap on your path forward.

It's important to get in the habit of doing these even when things are going well. Learning from successes and failures is how we constantly grow as teams.

Rewarding and recognizing individuals at a distance: So, like I say, treat everyone equally, until it's time to treat people special. No, I'm not contradicting myself. Sometimes people will excel and when they do, you want to recognize that, but the key to this is in how you do it.

When a team member has a victory, the whole team has won and the whole team should know who and why they're celebrating. Real-life example with names changed to protect the innocent, Carol manages a team of two dozen document processors, only four of whom are in the New England office. The rest work remotely, scattered throughout North America. She also manages another ten people who work out of an office in Eastern Europe, although their work is not connected to the work being done in the

West. Carol's company has something called a High-Five Program. Processors who excel are nominated for the award, given a $25 gift card, and entered into a monthly drawing for a bigger prize.

What's important is that all nominees are recognized publicly when the monthly winner is announced. This message goes to everyone on the team so that everyone can share in the celebration. Additionally, if the team beats their standard service levels for several documents processed or the number of errors detected, Carol sends the entire team a message congratulating everyone for their work along with a small gift.

Now, a couple of important things. Number one, you have to be very, very consistent in this.

If you send congratulations to one person, you have to send them to everyone who meets the same criteria. Failure to catch this will result in resentment, perception of favoritism, and assorted other evils.

The second thing is pretty obvious. If you need to call someone out on not performing, that's a private conversation. Public shaming is not a good recipe for team spirit. Of course, if it's team goals that were missed, it's okay to address that with the team, but be careful about ever singling one person out.

Another obvious point, but I'm going to mention it anyway, if your acknowledgement of individual success is accompanied by any kind of a concrete reward, a bonus, a gift card to Starbucks, a greeting card, or anything, you need to be sure that all similar successes are similarly rewarded.

Parity, parity, parity. I guarantee you that if you treat people differently, the team will find out and if the team finds out, that will damage the way they see you and hurt the way they think about the team.

CONCLUSION

As you are coming out of a crisis, I think it is really important not to say, "Phew, got that behind us". No, that did not end, and the road ahead is challenging, there are bigger and broader challenges. So, look at the broader implications of the crisis what you can do, and what crises you can anticipate. Back to the coronavirus crisis, Bill Gates laid this whole thing out. Now with that name of a pandemic in 2015 no one listened to him. So, can you be the leader that's going to perceive what are we looking for in the road ahead? And that›s important that you have that capacity and have that courage and have that insight and willingness to step up and say guys we got to focus on this.

It makes sense that the future would punish the hubris of a leader who believes something is certain when it is, in fact, out of their control. But the point about clarity is critically important. How do we have clarity about a future that promises to be more complex, crowded, and confusing than ever? For starters, you can have clarity about your values and beliefs. What do you value today? What will you stand up for both now and in the future? Where are you uncompromising? What is non-negotiable regardless of how the future plays out? Getting clarity on what you and those that you work with care about is critical, as it can inform tough decisions in murky territory.

Knowing what you care about allows you to stay focused on the why and adapt to the what and the how to get challenged.

9. Making the Shift from Individual Contributor to Team Manager: Letting Go of Old Mindsets

In the bustling city of Hyderabad, known for its rich history and burgeoning technology scene, there lived a dedicated professional named Anika. For years, Anika had thrived as an individual contributor at a leading IT company, where her technical prowess and commitment to excellence had earned her a stellar reputation.

But life has a way of presenting unexpected opportunities and challenges. One day, Anika received a call from her manager that would change the course of her career. She was offered a promotion to a team manager role, responsible for leading a group of talented engineers. It was a moment of great excitement mixed with apprehension, for the transition from an individual contributor to a team manager demanded more than just a change in job title; it required a profound shift in mindset.

As Anika embarked on this new journey, she was acutely aware of the challenges that lay ahead. The transition from being a top-performing individual contributor to a team manager required her to shift her focus from personal achievements to leading and supporting her team toward achieving collective goals. It was a shift that demanded a different set of skills, a different perspective, and an entirely different approach to work.

As she delved into this transformative journey, Anika knew she needed to equip herself with the right mindset and tools for success. Here are some of the strategies and tips she embraced along the way:

1. Develop a Team-First Mentality: Anika understood that the success of her team was now her top priority. It was no longer about individual accomplishments but about creating an environment where her team could thrive. She had to be willing to put the needs and aspirations of her team members above her own.

2. Build Trust with Your Team: Trust is the cornerstone of effective leadership. Anika knew she had to earn the trust of her team members. This meant being transparent, honest, and reliable in her interactions with them. She understood that trust was a fragile commodity that required constant nurturing.

3. Delegate Effectively: Anika quickly realized that she couldn't do it all herself. Delegation became her ally, allowing her to entrust important tasks to her team members. This not only empowered her team but also freed up her time to focus on broader strategic initiatives.

4. Develop Coaching and Mentoring Skills: Anika was passionate about helping her team members grow and reach their full potential. She invested time in developing her coaching and mentoring skills, providing guidance, constructive feedback, and unwavering support to each team member. Their success became her success.

5. Focus on Collaboration: Collaboration is the lifeblood of innovation in the tech industry. Anika recognized that her role was not just to manage individuals but to create an environment that encouraged collaboration and open communication. She embraced different perspectives and ideas, promoting a culture of teamwork and inclusivity.

6. Develop a Long-Term Perspective: Anika had always been oriented toward achieving short-term goals as an individual contributor. Now, as a manager, she needed to embrace a longer-term perspective. She learned to set strategic goals for her team, plan for the future, and balance these with the demands of the present.

Anika's journey into the world of team management was not without its challenges. She grappled with moments of self-doubt, faced resistance to change, and navigated the complexities of leading a diverse group of engineers. Yet, with unwavering determination and a commitment to her personal growth, she persevered.

One of the early lessons Anika learned was the importance of trust. As she settled into her new role, she realized that building and maintaining trust with her team members was paramount. To do this, she had to be transparent about her decisions, honest in her communication, and reliable in her actions. She also encouraged an open-door policy, allowing team members to express their concerns and ideas freely.

Delegation was another area where Anika had to adapt. As an individual contributor, she had become accustomed to taking on a multitude of tasks herself. Now, she needed to delegate effectively, entrusting her team members with responsibilities that aligned with their strengths and aspirations. This shift not only empowered her team but also allowed her to focus on strategic planning and guiding the team toward their goals.

Coaching and mentoring were skills that Anika actively cultivated. She recognized that her role was not just to manage her team but to facilitate their growth and development. She provided constructive feedback, offered guidance on career paths, and created a supportive environment for learning and improvement. As a result, her team members flourished, and their collective expertise grew stronger.

Collaboration became a centerpiece of Anika's managerial approach. She understood that the diverse talents of her team members could only reach their full potential through effective teamwork. Anika actively encouraged brainstorming sessions, cross-functional collaboration, and knowledge-sharing forums. She promoted an atmosphere where everyone's voice was valued, regardless of their role or experience level.

Anika's commitment to a long-term perspective was evident in her strategic planning. While she had previously focused on immediate tasks and goals, she now takes a broader view. She set ambitious yet achievable objectives for her team, aligning their efforts with the company's long-term vision. This approach allowed her to steer her team toward sustainable success.

Despite the challenges and uncertainties that came with her new role, Anika's journey as a team manager began to yield positive results. Her team members appreciated her team-first mentality, her trustworthiness, and her dedication to their growth. They thrived in an environment that encouraged collaboration, innovation, and a shared commitment to long-term success.

As months turned into years, Anika's team achieved remarkable milestones. Their projects garnered recognition, and their contributions to the company's success were undeniable. Anika herself continued to evolve as a leader, constantly refining her managerial skills and learning from her experiences.

Her story in the heart of Hyderabad became an inspiration to others facing similar transitions. Anika's journey demonstrated that with the right mindset and a dedication to continuous growth, one could successfully navigate the challenges of transitioning from an individual contributor to a team manager. Her legacy in the dynamic world of technology and business underscored the transformative power of leadership and the profound impact it could have on a team, an organization, and an entire industry.

10. Delegate to Elevate: How to Delegate Effectively and Achieve Your Goals

In the vibrant city of Bangalore, known as the Silicon Valley of India, where innovation echoed through the corridors of countless tech companies, there was a dedicated and accomplished manager named Raj. Raj had carved his path in the world of software development, rising through the ranks of a prominent IT firm. He had earned a reputation for his technical expertise and a unique leadership style that combined unwavering dedication with an innate ability to bring out the best in his team.

As his career progressed, Raj found himself at a crossroads—a juncture where his workload had swelled to a level that could only be described as daunting. Juggling multiple projects, overseeing a team of skilled engineers, and acting as a liaison with clients had become the norm. His plate was not merely full; it was overflowing, and the weight of responsibilities threatened to consume him.

In the midst of this whirlwind, Raj made a pivotal realization— one that would shape the trajectory of his career and leadership philosophy. He recognized that, while he had been proficient at taking on responsibilities and delivering results, he needed a different approach to sustain his success. He needed to unlock the power of delegation.

Delegation, Raj understood, was not merely a strategy to reduce his workload. It was a means to empower his team members, allowing them to take ownership of tasks and develop new skills. It was a way to foster a culture of collaboration and growth where each team member could contribute to their fullest potential.

Mastering the art of delegation became Raj's mission—a mission that would require a profound shift in his leadership style and a commitment to principles that would guide him on this transformative journey. These principles became his compass:

1. Identify the Right Tasks to Delegate: Raj recognized that effective delegation began with identifying the right tasks to delegate. He knew that not all responsibilities were suitable for delegation. Some tasks demanded his unique expertise and experience. To identify the right tasks, he meticulously assessed his workload, seeking those that could be entrusted to capable team members without compromising quality or efficiency.

2. Choose the Right Person for the Job: Once Raj had identified suitable tasks, he shifted his focus to selecting the right person for each job. It was crucial to match tasks with individuals who possessed the requisite skills and knowledge to complete them effectively. Equally important was ensuring that the chosen team members had the time and resources to take on additional responsibilities without jeopardizing their own commitments.

3. Clearly Communicate Expectations: Effective delegation hinges on clear communication of expectations. Raj understood that providing specific instructions and guidelines was paramount. He made it a point to outline the desired outcomes and the standards of quality that were expected. Clarity, he knew, was the linchpin of success in any delegated task.

4 Provide Necessary Support and Resources: To ensure that delegation was not just a handover but an investment in success, Raj recognized the importance of providing the necessary support and resources to his team members. This might involve granting access to tools or software, offering training or guidance, or providing ongoing support and feedback as needed. He viewed setting his team up for success as an integral part of his role as a manager.

5. Trust and Follow-Up: Trust was the cornerstone of effective delegation. Raj believed in trusting the individuals to whom he delegated tasks. He made a conscious effort to avoid micromanaging or interfering unnecessarily. Instead, he allowed his team members to take ownership of their assigned tasks, with the confidence that they would deliver as expected. However, trust did not equate to negligence. Raj recognized the importance of periodic follow-ups to ensure that tasks were progressing as planned and to offer support if needed.

Raj's journey into the realm of delegation was a deliberate one—a transformation that unfolded gradually but profoundly.

One day, as he was reviewing his ever-expanding workload, Raj came across a project that demanded immediate attention.

It involved developing a complex software module for a high-profile client. The project was not only time-sensitive but also required precision and technical finesse. Raj knew that this was the perfect opportunity to put his newfound delegation skills to the test.

After a thoughtful assessment, Raj selected Priya, a talented software engineer on his team, for the task. Priya had consistently demonstrated exceptional technical skills and a remarkable attention to detail in her previous assignments. Raj called her into his office to discuss the project.

"Priya," Raj began, "I have a project that's crucial for our client. It involves developing a complex software module, and I believe you're the perfect person for the job. I'll provide you with all the necessary resources and support, but I want you to take ownership of this project. I trust your skills and judgment, and I'm confident you can deliver."

Priya, feeling both honored and challenged, accepted the responsibility with a sense of determination. Raj proceeded to offer detailed instructions, outlining the client's requirements and the expected timeline. He also assured Priya that he was available for any guidance or support she might need along the way.

Over the next few weeks, Priya immersed herself in the project with unwavering enthusiasm and dedication. Drawing upon her technical expertise and creative problem-solving skills, she navigated through challenges and hurdles. Raj, true to his commitment to trust and follow-up, periodically checked in with Priya to discuss progress and provide any necessary guidance.

As the project neared completion, Priya had not only met but exceeded the client's expectations. The software module was not only delivered on time but also showcased innovative solutions that left the client thoroughly impressed.

Raj felt a profound sense of satisfaction—a testament to the power of delegation when executed with precision and trust. Delegating such a critical project had not only lightened his own workload but had also empowered Priya to shine and develop new skills. Priya, in turn, had gained confidence and a profound sense of ownership over her work.

Word of Priya's success spread like wildfire within the team and throughout the organization. Her accomplishment was celebrated not merely as a technical achievement but as a shining example of effective delegation and leadership in action.

Raj continued to refine his delegation skills, recognizing that it was an ongoing process. He found that by empowering his team members through delegation, he not only lightened his own load but also fostered a culture of growth, trust, and collaboration within his team. He encouraged his team members to take on new challenges and responsibilities, and he provided them with opportunities to expand their skills and expertise.

In the dynamic world of software development in Bangalore, Raj's journey as a manager who had mastered the art of delegation became a source of inspiration for many. His story illustrated that effective delegation was not merely about distributing tasks; it was about nurturing talent, fostering trust, and achieving collective success—a lesson that resonated with managers and leaders across industries in the bustling city.

Raj's commitment to delegation was not a one-time endeavor but a cornerstone of his leadership philosophy. He understood that by entrusting his team with responsibilities, he was not diminishing his own role but enhancing it. He was shaping a team of capable, motivated individuals who could collectively achieve greatness—a legacy that would endure long after the code was written and the projects.

11. Unconventional Pioneers: The Management Manifesto

In the bustling city of Mumbai, within the heart of a thriving IT company, there worked two managers with completely opposing philosophies. One was Rahul, a charismatic and spontaneous leader, and the other was Priya, a meticulous and planning-oriented manager. Their management styles couldn't have been more different, and it was this difference that would soon come to define their careers.

INTRODUCING RAHUL AND PRIYA

Rahul had always been a force to be reckoned with in the company. With his sharp wit, magnetic personality, and a seemingly endless supply of innovative ideas, he had risen through the ranks at an astonishing pace. His team adored him, not just for his professional acumen but also for his ability to make the workplace fun and engaging.

Priya, on the other hand, was known for her methodical approach to everything. She was the person who always had color-coded spreadsheets, detailed project plans, and a knack for foreseeing potential problems before they could escalate. Her desk was a testament to her dedication to planning, filled with charts, graphs, and Gantt charts.

Their paths crossed often at company meetings and brainstorming sessions, and it was evident to everyone that they were two sides of the same coin. While Rahul brought creativity and a sense of adventure to the table, Priya brought structure and a sense of security.

RAHUL'S SPONTANEITY

Rahul firmly believed in the power of spontaneity. He often said, "Life is too short to be bogged down by plans. You seize the day, and you make things happen." His philosophy wasn't just limited to his professional life; it extended into his personal life as well. He was known for his impromptu weekend getaways and surprise office parties that would pop up out of nowhere.

His team loved working with him. Every day was an adventure, and they thrived on the excitement and the feeling that anything was possible. Rahul's spontaneity seemed to work like magic. He could walk into a meeting with a vague idea and somehow turn it into a brilliant project that garnered praise from clients and colleagues alike.

PRIYA'S METHODICAL APPROACH

Priya, on the other hand, believed in meticulous planning. She often said, "A well-thought-out plan is the backbone of any successful endeavor." Her approach was systematic, and she approached every project with the mindset of an architect crafting a masterpiece.

Her team often found her approach to be overly cautious. They couldn't understand why she spent so much time planning when Rahul seemed to achieve great results with spontaneity. But Priya had seen the consequences of hasty decisions and the chaos that could ensue without a clear roadmap.

Her projects were known for their precision and reliability. Deadlines were always met, resources were never misallocated, and clients had a sense of security knowing that Priya was at the helm. But despite her successes, she couldn't help but feel that her colleagues viewed her as the "boring" manager who played it safe.

THE TURNING POINT

As the company continued to grow, Rahul's spontaneity began to show its limitations. What initially appeared as a flair for seizing opportunities turned into a series of missed deadlines, miscommunication, and strained client relationships. The projects that had once been the company's crown jewels were now plagued with issues, and morale among his team began to plummet.

Rahul found himself in a precarious position. He had to confront the fact that his spontaneous approach while exhilarating at times, was causing more harm than good. He knew he needed to make a change, but he wasn't sure how to do it without compromising his identity as a dynamic and innovative leader.

PRIYA'S ASCENSION

Meanwhile, Priya's star continued to rise. Her methodical planning and attention to detail were paying off more than ever. Her team had come to appreciate her structured approach, and they began to see the value in careful preparation. The projects she led were like well-oiled machines, and clients were singing her praises.

Priya, however, remained humble. She didn't revel in the success of her projects; instead, she focused on continually improving her planning methods. She knew that complacency was the enemy of progress, and she was determined to stay ahead of the curve.

THE GAME-CHANGING PROJECT

The defining moment for Rahul and Priya came when the company landed its biggest project to date. It was a massive client contract that had the potential to catapult them to new heights, but it also came with immense pressure and scrutiny. The entire company was invested in its success.

Rahul, ever the spontaneous visionary, insisted on taking the lead. He believed that his natural instinct for seizing opportunities would be the key to winning the client over. However, his team, scarred by past experiences, had reservations. They knew that this project required a level of precision and planning they hadn't seen from Rahul before.

Priya, who had been observing the situation closely, saw an opportunity to bridge the gap between spontaneity and planning. She offered to work with Rahul on the project, combining their strengths. Rahul, feeling the weight of the project's importance, agreed.

THE POWER OF COLLABORATION

The collaboration between Rahul and Priya was an eye-opener for both of them. Rahul saw the value of Priya's meticulous planning as they started to lay out the project's roadmap. Priya, in turn, learned to embrace Rahul's spontaneity as a source of creativity and innovation.

Together, they crafted a plan that was both structured and flexible. They defined clear roles and responsibilities, set achievable milestones, and established a system for regular progress updates. Rahul's ability to think on his feet became an asset in adapting to unexpected challenges, while Priya's planning ensured that they stayed on course.

THE SLOW CLIMB

The project kicked off with Rahul and Priya's combined approach at the helm. The initial excitement was palpable, but it was followed by intense scrutiny from the client. This project was a make-or-break moment for the company, and the pressure was immense.

At first, it seemed like Rahul's spontaneous approach might prevail. His ability to charm clients and come up with innovative solutions on the spot was evident. However, as the project progressed, the cracks began to show. Deadlines were missed, resources were strained, and communication among team members started to falter.

PRIYA'S RESURGENCE

As the project teetered on the brink of disaster, Rahul knew he had to make a difficult decision. He turned to Priya for help, acknowledging that her planning expertise was needed to salvage the situation. Priya agreed to step in, but she made it clear that they needed to adhere to a well-structured plan.

Over the next few weeks, Priya and her team worked tirelessly. They redefined roles, clarified expectations, and implemented a rigorous tracking system. The project slowly but steadily started to turn around. Deadlines were met, communication improved, and client satisfaction began to rise.

SUCCESS AGAINST THE ODDS

In the end, the project was a resounding success. The company not only retained its client but also received accolades for its professionalism and efficiency. Rahul, once a staunch believer in spontaneity, had learned the invaluable lesson that planning was the foundation for every successful journey. He began to embrace the importance of careful preparation and started incorporating it into his management style.

The story of Rahul and Priya became a legend in the company. It served as a powerful reminder that while spontaneity had its place, it was planning that truly created the roadmap to success. In the bustling world of Mumbai's corporate landscape, the tale of Rahul and Priya was a testament to the enduring power of thoughtful preparation in the workplace.

THE TRANSFORMATION OF RAHUL

The success of the game-changing project had a profound impact on Rahul. It was a turning point in his career, and he found himself reevaluating his management philosophy. He realized that spontaneity, while a valuable trait, needed to be harnessed within the framework of planning for sustained success.

Rahul sought guidance from Priya, who had become not just a colleague but also a mentor and friend. Priya, always open to sharing her knowledge, welcomed Rahul's willingness to learn. She introduced him to the intricacies of strategic planning, helping him understand how to identify key objectives, allocate resources effectively, and anticipate potential roadblocks.

As Rahul absorbed these lessons, he noticed a transformation in his leadership style. He became more methodical in his approach, taking the time to analyze data and market trends before making decisions. His once-impulsive nature gave way to a more measured and calculated demeanor.

THE RISE OF PRIYA

Priya's reputation within the company continued to soar. Her expertise in planning and project management made her an indispensable asset to the organization. She was often tapped to lead critical projects, and her meticulous attention to detail was celebrated by both clients and colleagues.

However, Priya remained committed to personal growth. She recognized that leadership was not static and that there was always room for improvement. She attended leadership seminars, sought out mentors of her own, and delved into the nuances of team dynamics and motivational strategies.

In her pursuit of excellence, Priya also took the time to mentor junior managers within the company. She shared her knowledge of effective planning and instilled in them the importance of meticulous preparation. Her guidance created a ripple effect throughout the organization, as more managers adopted a balanced approach to leadership.

THE NEW WORKPLACE PARADIGM

The transformation of Rahul and the continued success of Priya had a profound impact on the company's culture. The once-clear divide between spontaneity and planning began to blur as managers and employees alike embraced the idea that both approaches had their merits.

Cross-functional teams formed, bringing together individuals with diverse skill sets and management philosophies. The company began to encourage open dialogue and collaboration, recognizing that the synergy between different perspectives could lead to innovation and efficiency.

The organization also invested in training programs that emphasized the importance of strategic planning while encouraging creativity and adaptability. Employees were empowered to think critically, anticipate challenges, and develop contingency plans. The workplace was no longer a battleground between spontaneity and planning; it had become a fertile ground for balanced leadership.

NAVIGATING FUTURE CHALLENGES

As the IT company continued to thrive, it faced new challenges in an ever-evolving industry. Rapid technological advancements, changing client demands, and global economic shifts created an environment that required nimble responses and forward-thinking strategies.

Rahul and Priya, now considered the company's dynamic duo, were at the forefront of navigating these challenges. Their ability to combine spontaneity and planning made them uniquely suited to lead the organization through turbulent times. They recognized that while planning provided a steady course, spontaneity allowed for quick course corrections when needed.

The lessons they had learned from their collaborative success were put to the test time and again. They led their teams with confidence, adapting to the changing landscape while maintaining a firm commitment to their core values of preparation and innovation.

THE IMPACT BEYOND THE COMPANY

Word of Rahul and Priya's success story spread beyond the confines of their organization. They were invited to speak at industry conferences and seminars, where they shared their journey and the lessons they had learned. Their story became an inspiration to managers and leaders in various sectors, not just in Mumbai but across India.

Their emphasis on the symbiotic relationship between spontaneity and planning resonated with leaders facing similar challenges in a rapidly evolving world. Rahul and Priya's insights influenced management philosophies in companies far and wide, fostering a culture of adaptability and resilience.

THE LEGACY LIVES ON

As Rahul and Priya continued to lead their company to new heights, they never forgot the lessons they had learned during their transformative journey. They remained committed to personal growth and the development of their teams. They knew that leadership was a continuous journey, and they embraced every opportunity to learn and evolve.

Their collaborative approach became a hallmark of their leadership, setting the tone for the entire organization. They encouraged their teams to think critically, plan meticulously, and be open to seizing opportunities when they arose. The workplace had evolved into a dynamic and balanced ecosystem where innovation thrived, and success was a collective effort.

CONCLUSION - THE LEGACY ENDURES

In the bustling city of Mumbai, where dreams and opportunities intersected, the story of Rahul and Priya became a timeless tale of leadership and growth. Their journey from polar opposites to collaborative leaders served as a reminder that success in the workplace required a delicate balance between spontaneity and planning.

Their legacy endured not only within their organization but also in the hearts and minds of leaders across the country. Their story was a testament to the enduring power of adaptability, resilience, and the willingness to learn from one another.

As the IT company they had helped transform continued to thrive, Rahul and Priya looked to the future with a sense of optimism. They knew that the ever-changing landscape of the workplace would continue to present challenges and opportunities. Still, armed with the lessons of their past, they were confident that they could navigate any path that lay ahead, forging a brighter and more successful tomorrow.

12. Unleashing Potential: Strategies for Hiring Women in Leadership Roles

Despite significant progress in the realm of diversity and inclusion, the hiring of women in middle and senior leadership positions remains a pervasive challenge. While numerous female leaders have proven their capabilities and worth, the inclusion of women in these critical roles is still sporadic. Organizations often express apprehension, doubting the commitment and suitability of women for these positions. Concerns range from assumptions that women may prioritize family and children over their careers to doubts about their ability to navigate complex negotiations or withstand high-pressure situations. Furthermore, the safety needs of women in the workplace differ significantly from those of their male counterparts. These and other challenges persist, hindering the progress toward gender equality in leadership positions.

To address this disparity, organizations must take deliberate steps to increase the hiring of women in middle and senior leadership roles. They must recognize that the success of their business depends on leveraging the diverse perspectives, skills, and experiences that women bring to the table. Moreover, women themselves need to assert their capabilities and prove their worth as serious contenders for these positions. By bridging the gap between aspiration and reality, both organizations and women can work together to achieve greater gender balance in leadership.

This article delves into the strategies and actions necessary to overcome the barriers that limit the hiring of women in middle and senior leadership roles. It explores the steps that organizations can take to promote gender diversity, as well as the actions women can adopt to position themselves as strong candidates. By addressing biases, fostering inclusive cultures, implementing targeted development programs, emphasizing leadership competencies, cultivating support networks, advocating for oneself, and addressing implicit bias in selection processes, organizations and women can drive transformative change in the workplace.

The time for change is now. It is imperative to break down the barriers that impede the progress of women in leadership positions and create an environment where gender equality thrives. By embracing the talent, perspectives, and capabilities of women, organizations will not only unlock new avenues for success but also set an example for future generations. Together, let us embark on a journey to increase the hiring of women in middle and senior leadership roles and build a more inclusive, equitable, and prosperous future.

Challenge Biases and Stereotypes: Addressing biases and stereotypes is crucial for creating a fair and inclusive hiring process. Organizations should invest in training programs that raise awareness of unconscious biases and their impact on decision-making. By educating hiring managers and decision-makers, they can recognize and mitigate biases that may influence their judgments. Implementing blind recruitment practices, such as removing gender identifiers from resumes, ensures that candidates are evaluated solely on their qualifications and skills.

Foster an Inclusive Organizational Culture: Organizations need to foster an inclusive culture that supports work-life balance and gender equality. This involves implementing policies and practices that accommodate the diverse needs of employees. Offering flexible working arrangements, parental leave, and childcare support enables women to balance their professional and personal responsibilities effectively. By creating an environment that values and supports employees' well-being, organizations attract and retain talented women who can contribute to leadership positions.

Implement Targeted Talent Development Programs: To increase the pool of qualified women for middle and senior leadership roles, organizations should implement targeted talent development programs. These programs provide women with opportunities for skill enhancement, leadership training, and access to mentors and sponsors. By investing in the professional growth and advancement of women, organizations signal their commitment to fostering gender diversity at the highest levels of leadership.

Emphasize Leadership Competencies and Potential: Organizations should focus on assessing leadership competencies and potential rather than solely relying on past experiences and qualifications. Women bring unique perspectives, skills, and capabilities to the table. By broadening the criteria for leadership positions, organizations can identify individuals with the right leadership qualities, regardless of their background or industry. This approach ensures that diverse talents and experiences are valued and considered in the hiring process.

Cultivate supportive networks and allies: Building a supportive network is vital for women's advancement in leadership roles. Organizations should establish mentorship programs, pair women with senior leaders, and create networking platforms. These initiatives provide women with guidance, support, and opportunities to connect with influential professionals. Additionally, allies within the organization, both male and female, can advocate for gender equality, provide sponsorship, and help break down barriers to advancement.

Advocate for Yourself and Showcase Achievements: Women must take an active role in advocating for themselves and showcasing their achievements. They should confidently communicate their accomplishments, skills, and ambitions. Actively seeking out challenging assignments, demonstrating the ability to handle difficult negotiations or stressful situations, and taking on leadership opportunities within projects or cross-functional teams are ways to showcase their capabilities. By proactively highlighting their contributions, women demonstrate their readiness for leadership roles.

Addressing Implicit Bias in Selection Processes: Organizations need to examine their selection processes and policies to identify and address implicit bias. This includes reviewing job descriptions for gendered language and ensuring they are inclusive and unbiased. Diversifying interview panels can provide diverse perspectives and minimize bias. Implementing structured interview techniques that focus on assessing competencies and potential rather than personal characteristics ensures a fair evaluation. By eliminating implicit bias, organizations create equal opportunities for all candidates.

The hiring of women in middle and senior leadership roles remains a persistent challenge despite the progress made in promoting diversity and inclusion. Organizations must recognize that gender diversity in leadership is not only a matter of equality but also a driver of innovation and success. By actively addressing biases and stereotypes, fostering an inclusive organizational culture, implementing targeted talent development programs, emphasizing leadership competencies and potential, cultivating supportive networks and allies, advocating for oneself, and addressing implicit bias in selection processes, companies can make significant strides toward increasing the hiring of women in leadership positions.

It is essential for organizations to challenge the biases and stereotypes that hinder gender equality. By raising awareness of unconscious biases and implementing blind recruitment practices, organizations can ensure a fair evaluation of candidates based on their qualifications and skills. Creating an inclusive culture that supports work-life balance, offers flexibility, and provides parental leave support is crucial for attracting and retaining talented women.

Furthermore, targeted talent development programs play a vital role in nurturing the pipeline of qualified women for leadership roles. By investing in their professional growth and providing access to mentors and sponsors, organizations demonstrate their commitment to supporting women's advancement.

Women themselves must assert their qualifications, showcase their achievements, and actively seek out challenging opportunities to position themselves as serious contenders for leadership roles.

By advocating for their abilities and ambitions, women can break down barriers and overcome biases that may hinder their progress.

In the journey toward increasing the hiring of women in middle and senior leadership roles, collaboration between organizations and women themselves is crucial. It requires a collective effort to challenge existing norms, foster inclusive cultures, and provide equal opportunities for all qualified candidates.

By embracing diversity and creating environments where women can thrive, organizations will unlock the full potential of their talent pool, drive innovation, and achieve greater success. It is time to shatter the glass ceiling, empower women to take on leadership roles and create a future where gender equality in leadership is the norm rather than the exception. Together, we can forge a path toward a more inclusive and equitable world.

13. Glass Ceilings and Golden Dreams: A Woman's Journey in the Corporate World

The city of Mumbai, with its sprawling skyline of towering glass and steel, pulsated with energy and ambition. It was a city where dreams clashed with reality, where fortunes were made and lives were shaped. In this metropolis, among the myriad stories of aspiration and triumph, lived a young woman named Meera.

From her earliest days, Meera had carried a spark of determination within her that would one day set her on an extraordinary path. She was born into a middle-class family in a modest neighborhood, where the echoes of ambition reverberated through the narrow alleyways. Her parents, both teachers, instilled in her a deep appreciation for education and a fervent belief in the power of knowledge.

Growing up, Meera excelled academically. Her sharp intellect and unwavering dedication soon distinguished her as a standout student. It was evident that she possessed a rare combination of talent and tenacity that promised a future filled with promise.

As she approached her teenage years, Meera's dreams crystallized. She knew she wanted to pursue a career in finance, a field where she believed she could make her mark. With unwavering determination, she embarked on the arduous journey of preparing for the competitive entrance exams that would secure her a place in a prestigious business school.

The path to her dream was not easy. Late-night study sessions, rigorous test preparations, and a relentless pursuit of excellence became her companions. She faced skepticism from some who questioned whether a girl from her background could excel in a field dominated by men. However, Meera's resolve remained unshaken.

Her hard work paid off when she earned a place in one of Mumbai's top business schools. It was a moment of triumph not just for her but for her family, who had watched her with pride as she transformed her dreams into reality.

Meera's journey was only just beginning. Armed with a degree in finance and an unyielding spirit, she was ready to take on the world. Her story would soon intersect with the challenging landscape of the Indian corporate world, where her talent and determination would be tested in ways she could never have anticipated.

THE BALANCING ACT

As Meera's career progressed, she faced the immense challenge of balancing her professional aspirations with her family responsibilities. This was an issue that many of her male colleagues did not fully grasp. While they could focus solely on their careers, Meera had to navigate the intricate dance of juggling multiple roles.

Her days often began with high-stakes client meetings, followed by a mad dash to pick up her son from school. Evenings blurred into a frenetic whirlwind of cooking dinner, assisting with homework, and managing household chores—all after a grueling day at the office. Meera was living the reality of the "second shift," the expectation that women bear the majority of caregiving responsibilities.

The pressure to fulfill both her professional and familial roles was immense, and it often left her physically and emotionally drained. Despite this, Meera was determined not to let these challenges deter her from her goals.

THE MOTHERHOOD PENALTY

As Meera continued to excel in her career, she encountered another formidable obstacle: the motherhood penalty. This penalty was a stark reality for women in the corporate world. Employers often held biases that assumed mothers would be less committed to their jobs and, therefore, less deserving of promotions and pay raises.

This bias manifested subtly but significantly in Meera's career. She observed that her male counterparts received more high-profile assignments and were more frequently considered for leadership positions, while she occasionally found herself sidelined. The assumption that motherhood somehow diminished her dedication to her career was a constant source of frustration.

Despite these obstacles, Meera remained unwavering in her resolve. She knew that her worth as a professional should not be defined by her motherhood status. She continued to shine in her role, gaining the respect and admiration of her clients and colleagues.

HARASSMENT AND MISCONDUCT

In the world of corporate life, another significant challenge women like Meera often faced was harassment and misconduct. Even in respected companies, instances of harassment and inappropriate behavior by male colleagues or superiors were unfortunately not uncommon, creating a hostile work environment for women.

Meera's encounter with harassment was both shocking and distressing. During a critical presentation to a potential client, her male manager, Mr. Khanna, made an inappropriate comment that sent shockwaves through her. It was a veiled suggestion that her career could advance faster if she were willing to engage in an unethical "cooperation" with him.

Meera was deeply appalled by Mr. Khanna's behavior. It was a pivotal moment that forced her to confront the harsh reality that many women faced in corporate life. She knew that compromising her values and integrity for career advancement was not an option, regardless of how tempting the offer might have seemed to some.

TAKING A STAND

Meera made a courageous decision to take a stand against harassment. She reported Mr. Khanna's misconduct to the company's Human Resources department and sought guidance from the firm's legal team. This decision was not without its challenges; she was aware of the potential backlash and the toll it might take on her career. However, Meera believed deeply in the importance of standing up against harassment.

The subsequent investigation was thorough and painstaking. Meera had to provide evidence and share her account of the incident in detail. Her male colleagues watched closely, with some offering their support for her brave actions while others engaged in whispered conversations behind her back. Meera had become a symbol of resilience and determination for women throughout the company.

With the support of concrete evidence and her unwavering commitment to justice, Mr. Khanna was held accountable for his actions. His termination sent a powerful message throughout the company: harassment would not be tolerated.

THE RIPPLE EFFECT

Meera's story did not end with Mr. Khanna's departure from the company; it was just the beginning. Her journey, her courage to confront harassment head-on, and her commitment to justice had a profound impact on the corporate culture within her workplace.

Her male colleagues began to reflect on their own actions and attitudes, leading to a significant shift in behavior and attitudes within the workplace. The company used her case as an opportunity to reevaluate its policies and practices concerning harassment and discrimination, marking the onset of a more inclusive and equitable work environment.

Word of Meera's story began to circulate not just within her company but throughout the corporate world in India. She became an advocate for gender equality, speaking at industry events and mentoring young women entering the field. Her actions had a lasting and transformative effect on the corporate landscape.

THE CLIMB CONTINUES

As Meera continued to advance in her career, she did not forget the challenges she had faced along the way. She used her position to create more opportunities for women within her company, advocating for diversity and inclusion initiatives that would level the playing field for all.

Her commitment to equality and her exemplary rise through the corporate ranks became an inspiration to countless women who aspired to break barriers in the Indian corporate setup. She proved that it was indeed possible to reach the pinnacle of her career without compromising one's values and ethics.

A BEACON OF HOPE

Meera's journey became a beacon of hope in the corporate world. Her story inspired change not only within her own company but also in the broader corporate landscape of India. Women across the country found the courage to speak out against discrimination and harassment, realizing that their voices could make a significant difference.

The impact of Meera's actions extended far beyond the confines of her workplace. Companies across India began to reevaluate their policies and practices, recognizing the importance of creating inclusive and equitable environments. Gender diversity at all levels of the corporate hierarchy became a priority.

THE FUTURE BECKONS

As Meera looked toward the future, she saw a different landscape unfolding. The corporate world in India was slowly but steadily changing. The biases and barriers that had plagued women for generations were gradually eroding, replaced by a growing commitment to gender equality.

Women like Meera were no longer viewed as exceptions but as leaders and trailblazers. The rise of women in leadership roles served as a testament to their capabilities and the critical role of diversity in decision-making.

A NEW DAWN

Meera's journey in the Indian corporate world had been one of triumph over adversity, a testament to the strength and resilience of women in the face of formidable challenges. Her story had sparked a movement, one that would continue to break down barriers and shatter glass ceilings for generations to come.

As the sun set over Mumbai's skyline, casting a warm, golden glow over the city, Meera knew that her journey was far from over. She had paved the way for others, and she was determined to continue making a difference. In the new dawn of India's corporate world, women like Meera were rising, and the future held boundless possibilities.

A SHINING BEACON

Meera's journey through the challenging terrain of the Indian corporate world had been an awe-inspiring tale of resilience, fortitude, and unwavering determination. From her humble beginnings in a modest neighborhood to her ascent through the ranks of a prestigious financial firm, her story had captured the hearts and minds of many.

As the years rolled on, Meera's influence continued to grow. She had become a guiding light, a shining beacon of hope for countless young women who aspired to break through the barriers that had once held her back. Her story was no longer just her own; it had become an inspiration that echoed across boardrooms and college campuses alike.

Meera's impact extended far beyond the walls of her office. The corporate landscape in India was undergoing a transformation. Companies were recognizing the importance of diversity and inclusion, and Meera had played a pivotal role in bringing about this change. Gender diversity at all levels of the corporate hierarchy was no longer a mere aspiration; it was a tangible goal that companies were actively pursuing.

But Meera's journey was not just about breaking glass ceilings and achieving professional success. It was a testament to the enduring power of dreams, the relentless pursuit of excellence, and the unshakable belief in oneself. It was proof that no obstacle, no bias, and no adversity could stifle the aspirations of those who dared to dream big.

As the sun dipped below the Mumbai skyline, casting a warm, golden glow over the city, Meera stood on her office balcony, reflecting on her journey. She knew that her mission was far from over. There were still challenges to be faced, battles to be fought, and barriers to be torn down. But she faced the future with the same indomitable spirit that had carried her this far.

Meera's story had become a timeless tale of triumph—a testament to the extraordinary potential that lay within each of us, waiting to be unleashed. It was a reminder that, in the pursuit of our dreams, there were no limits, no boundaries, and no obstacles that could withstand the power of determination.

And so, as the city of Mumbai continued to pulse with ambition and aspiration, Meera's story would forever be etched in its vibrant tapestry, inspiring generations to come to reach for the stars and, in doing so, change the world.

14. HR Digitalization – Embracing the Future

Technology is here and is revolutionizing the world, making relentless change the only constant. In the Digital Darwinism era that we live in today, organizations that do not adapt to these technology-led changes will find themselves on the path to extinction. And those who adapt in an agile fashion will thrive amid aggressive competition and cluttered markets. While digitalization and digital transformation efforts have been strong on the consumer and business processes fronts, digitalization of the HR function has been largely lacking.

Things are changing post-Covid. Earlier, only parts of recruitment and performance appraisal were digitalized while other areas of human resource management weren't. After the pandemic, several organizations have gone digital in areas such as new employee onboarding, employee engagement, learning and development, job interviews, employee documentation, etc.

However, there still exist organizations that have not prioritized HR digitalization or are still not thinking beyond recruitment. This is especially the case with SMEs (small and medium enterprises) who do not prioritize HR digitalization owing to their frugal resources and budgetary constraints.

Given that traditional HR methods are failing, can such organizations thrive in the new workplace norm where a majority of the workforce will either work remotely or in hybrid work environments? What are the consequences of not digitalizing the HR function and focusing solely on other business processes? How can organizations start/bolster HR digital transformation? Keep reading to find out.

HR DIGITALIZATION: AN INTRODUCTION

HR digitalization is the process of leveraging digital technologies such as cloud computing, automation, analytics, AI, ML, social media, mobile technologies, etc., for the modernization of operational HR processes, making them more efficient, agile, data-driven, collaborative, and people-centric. It leads to superior employee experiences, better performance, and sustainable business growth.

So, is it just about transforming paperwork into spreadsheets or digitizing records? Most definitely not!

DIGITIZATION VS. DIGITALIZATION

Digitization and digitalization are often assumed to be one and the same, but they are different. Digitization is simply the process of transferring material things into digital things. For instance, taking physical employee records and converting them into digital copies.

Digitalization of HR is a much more complex process that requires organizations to thoughtfully rethink HR processes and adopt technology to solve people's challenges within the organization. In other words, it requires the organization to reimagine how work is done. HR digitalization is not a technology-driven challenge but a people-oriented one.

While HR digitization is a good practice and a seemingly quick fix, it will not usher in the kind of reinvention and modernization necessary to thrive in the remote and hybrid world of work. Organizations must focus on HR digitalization to create collaborative, unified, and comprehensive digital workplaces equipped with advanced technology to bolster productivity, efficiency, and business outcomes.

WHAT DOES HR DIGITALIZATION ENTAIL?

It is important to note that HR digitalization is not just about automation. While automation of repetitive, manual, and low-value tasks to free up employee bandwidth is an important component of HR digitalization, it cannot be the only component. Automation is not adequate to modernize HR processes as it creates repeatable, self-service HR transactions that are often disconnected and even outdated.

HR digitalization needs to have an integrated, holistic, and intelligent approach to solving HR challenges and modernizing the way people work. It needs to help create meaningful and challenging work. The tools introduced must be purposeful and relevant. Instead of creating disjunct experiences and siloed departments, HR digitalization must foster a culture of innovation, creativity, and collaboration, enabling the workforce to drive business outcomes.

THE STAGES OF HR DIGITALIZATION

Stage 1: Business as usual

Stage 2: Present and Active is the stage of experimentation with new technology within the organization while driving digital literacy.

Stage 3: Formalization stage, where the business relevance is analyzed and irrelevant digital technologies are (or should be) eliminated.

Stage 4: People realize the power of technology-led collaboration, shared efforts, and insights. This leads to the development of new strategic roadmaps.

Stage 5: The convergence stage is where digital transformation teams are formed to guide the strategic and operational efforts of the organization.

Stage 6: Digitalization and digital transformation become an established norm in the ecosystem and the new 'business as usual'.

THE IMPORTANCE AND BENEFITS OF HR DIGITALIZATION

STRENGTHENS AND FUTURE-PROOFS THE RECRUITMENT PROCESS

One of the critical focus areas of HR is recruitment since it determines the quality of talent within the organization and, thus, the business outcomes. HR digitalization enables organizations to effectively strengthen and future-proof their recruitment process by helping attract and retain the best talent in the competitive labor market.

Organizations can create fast, comprehensive, and intelligent recruitment systems with the help of technologies like AI, intelligent automation, predictive analytics, self-learning systems, mobile technologies, etc. This way, they can streamline and make their pre-recruitment processes more effective and data-driven.

The application process can be made hassle-free through mobile apps. Profile scanning and shortlisting can be made faster and error-free through automation based on preset parameters. More personalized and authentic onboarding experiences can be created using AI-driven tools. Organizations can also leverage gamification and social media platforms such as LinkedIn to improve the prospects of hiring the right candidates.

ENHANCE HR PROCESS EFFICIENCY

With automated and centralized HR tools, HR processes such as leave management, payroll management, administrative tasks, etc. can be fast-tracked with minimal human intervention and errors. So, employees, managers, and HR teams do not have to engage in wasteful and arduous processes for simple things like applying for leave. While improving efficiency and business outcomes, it offers significant cost and time savings.

CENTRALIZATION OF DATA

Digital HR tools enables organizations to aggregate and centralize employee data from multiple, siloed channels into one, unified platform. This ensures greater visibility into employee performance and the lifecycle. The HR team or managers can simply access records with a few clicks rather than scouring through thousands of paper files to find the necessary information.

ENABLES SWIFT, DATA-DRIVEN HR DECISIONS

Digital HR tools and software offer real-time, accurate, actionable insights to relevant people to make data-driven, swift decisions. These insights empower HR teams to strengthen processes such as performance appraisals, recruitment, learning and development, employee engagement, and so on.

BOOSTS EMPLOYEE PRODUCTIVITY

By fostering greater collaboration, using agile processes, and eliminating manual drudgery, digital HR tools help boost employee productivity. They can focus on high-value and core activities rather than spending massive amounts of time and resources on low-value, manual, and repetitive tasks.

For instance, AI-powered self-service tools, chatbots, and AI-powered digital assistants free up HR bandwidth significantly as employees can resolve queries by themselves. The intervention of HR professionals may be necessary only for complex queries and requests that the AI-powered tool cannot handle. From the employee perspective, support is available 24x7 and instantly. So, they do not have to wait for hours or days before their queries are resolved.

ELEVATES EMPLOYEE EXPERIENCES

HR digitalization helps organizations make work more meaningful and challenging for employees. So, employees don't have to begrudgingly sit through manual drudgery that does not require their expertise or specialized skill sets. It enables smoother collaboration between a globally dispersed workforce. Further, HR digitalization helps make HR processes more agile, responsive, and frictionless.

Through cloud-based apps, collaboration tools, smarter integrations, AI-powered tools, and so on, organizations can craft personalized, authentic, and seamless employee experiences.

WHY IS HR DIGITALIZATION NECESSARY IN THE NEW WORKPLACE NORM?

While the COVID-19 pandemic gave the much-needed push for the digital transformation of organizations and their HR functions, the changing demographics of the workforce, globalization, and the advent of newer technology have also been dramatically changing the work world.

Today, geography and physical locations are starting to wane in importance as opposed to the need for flexibility, efficiency, and agility. The result is that remote and hybrid work models are becoming the new workplace norm.

In the new workplace norm, with a growing number of remote and geographically dispersed employees, traditional HR policies, practices, and processes are failing. Collaborative, digital work cultures are critical for business continuity and growth. Further, there is a strong need to be agile to adapt quickly to the fast-paced changes in the work world and otherwise thrive in the era of Digital Darwinism. HR digitalization makes all this possible in the new workplace norm.

Employers who are invested in modernization and digital transformation will thrive in the future of work and remain competitive in the labor and product markets. And those organizations that do not prioritize HR digitalization now will start losing their competitive edge and, over time, their relevance.

WAYS DIGITAL HR CAN BE LEVERAGED IN THE NEW ERA

- Cloud-based human capital management (HCM) systems for integrated, deep HR functionalities in one place.

- Performance management systems that allow hassle-free performance tracking, real-time sharing of feedback, and so on to help engage and retain critical talent.

- People analytics tools analyze and predict employee behavior, enabling organizations to take preemptive action to avert crises, including health and safety issues.

- Process automation for repetitive, manual tasks such as filling out forms, leave applications, vacation approvals, etc.

- Using augmented reality (AR), virtual reality (VR), AI, ML, and analytics to improve learning and development outcomes.

- AI-powered software, gamification, and mobile apps for future-ready recruitment.

- AI-powered helpdesks, digital assistants, and chatbots to enable the self-serving of HR queries.

- Recommendation engines offer relevant course suggestions to help employees upskill themselves.

HOW TO START OR BOLSTER YOUR DIGITAL HR EFFORTS?

THE CHALLENGES

One of the top challenges in an organization's HR digitalization efforts is resistance from the C-suite to modernize. This leads to a lack of adequate budgets for HR digitalization and an inability to invest in critical HR technology. Without C-suite buy-in, employee buy-in is challenging. Without people accepting and adopting HR tools and technology, the investment would only be wasted.

The second critical challenge is the lack of agility to make iterations to improve outcomes. This is often the case when organizations build solutions top-down and roll them out. This leaves no scope for employee feedback or improvements.

Thirdly, the lack of proper goals and objectives is yet another challenge in bolstering HR digitalization efforts. This would often lead to organizations investing in the wrong technology or automating the wrong processes. And their outcomes would suffer.

THE STRATEGIES TO START YOUR HR DIGITALIZATION JOURNEY

- Clearly define goals, objectives, and priorities before embarking on the HR digitalization journey.
- Identify who will run the HR digitalization processes and hire additional resources, if necessary.
- Identify HR processes that can be digitalized and prioritize them.
- Get executive buy-in by presenting a well-researched and meaningful business case.
- Create a culture of digitalization.
- Choose the right tools and software.
- Technology should be used as an enabler, not the end goal.
- Offer greater autonomy and flexibility to employees using AI-powered assistants and self-service platforms.
- The technology and solutions used must be flexible and allow iterations.
- Define KPIs and metrics. Use these to improve outcomes and ensure that the goals are achieved.

MOVING FORWARD...

HR digitalization is not optional anymore. If you want to thrive in the future of work, you must start your HR digitalization journey now!

15. New Outlook Toward Employee Compensation & Benefits

Remote work was an option for employees for short time periods in only a few companies. But the COVID-19 pandemic has brought remote work into the mainstream. Several organizations were forced to adopt it, rather hastily, when the pandemic hit. Over the past two years, organizations have experienced firsthand the many benefits of remote work, including productivity gains, cost savings, and long-term value creation.

Several employees are looking to shift to companies with more flexible work options when their current employers aren't able to provide remote work opportunities. Further, experts believe that in the post-pandemic reality, we are headed toward a hybrid work world, with organizations having a mix of remote and on-premises workforces. So, there is a higher adoption of remote work among organizations of all kinds.

Today, formal remote work policies and strategies exist as a result of conscious restructuring and redesign by organizations. This is to ensure the retention of the workforce and its critical talent in the present and in the future.

One of the key challenges facing organizations in this shift to remote and hybrid work environments is to have better-suited compensation and benefits strategies. Force-fitting traditional compensation and benefits will only be counterproductive. Why?

Benefits that were considered the gold standard in traditional work culture may not hold any value today or in the future. Accordingly, organizations have been looking to reshape and transform their compensation and benefits to ensure that the total package is able to retain key talent and attract the right talent moving forward.

In this article, we take a look at the transforming compensation and benefits strategies and the employee rewards that should and shouldn't feature in compensation and benefits moving forward.

SHIFTING PAY STRATEGIES

Over the course of the pandemic, we saw employees migrating away from expensive urban locations and commercial areas of metropolitan cities to smaller towns and rural areas. Thanks to the remote work forced by the pandemic, they weren't required to stay close to the office just to hold onto their high-paying jobs. Several of them intend to stay where they are and work remotely.

Companies are facing a new conundrum as a result. Should they pay remote workers in affordable locations the same salaries as those who remain in the expensive commercial hubs? Should employees working remotely take a pay cut? Should the location of the employees be factored into compensation considerations? What other factors should the company consider in deciding the pay and total rewards package for an employee?

WAYS IN WHICH PAY STRATEGIES ARE SHIFTING FOR REMOTE WORKERS

Data suggests that 81% of employers still lack effective pay strategies for remote workers. Among the organizations with formal pay strategies for remote workers, the following approaches have emerged:

- **Salaries based on the employee's location:**

  Facebook is one of the companies that has gone this way. Having allowed employees to go fully remote, the company has set employee pay scales based on the cost of living in their location. Their location would be monitored using internal employee logs. Employees who have moved out of Silicon Valley into more affordable locations may see a nominal salary cut.

  Payment platform Stripe offered a bonus of USD 20,000 to its employees to leave San Francisco and move to affordable locations, with the caveat that they would take a 10% pay cut from their base salary.

- **Setting a pay scale based on the closest regional office or reporting office:**

  Another strategy being adopted is to set salaries based on the going market rates in the location of the closest regional office that employees report to.

  Mural, a visual collaboration company, took a novel approach to creating zones and setting the pay scale for employees based on the zone in which they fell. For instance, the Bay Area and Greater New York areas will have the highest pay scale, while those in Nashville or Atlanta will fall on the lower rungs of compensation. They revisit their compensation strategies every six months to make necessary adjustments and be on par with the market.

- **Setting a pay scale based on the location of the main office:**

This is another approach adopted by several companies, wherein the pay scale of the employees is set the same regardless of their location. This pay scale is based on the location of the main office. This helps organizations boost their diversity and inclusion initiatives while being able to recruit the best talent, no matter where they are located.

This approach also helps organizations prevent feelings of resentment that employees receiving lower pay for the same work may have. This helps ensure that organizational culture and employee experience do not suffer.

Reddit has adopted this approach and done away with its geographical compensation zones in 2021. It pays all its employees Bay Area-level salaries. Given the different trade-offs employees must consider while deciding where to live, the company believes this decision will offer flexibility and support employees need in making the decision.

This approach is beneficial even for companies located outside the high-cost commercial hubs. They can pay their employees based on local standards rather than matching up to the high market rates, say in New York, where a remote employee may be located.

- **Salaries based on the national pay average and adjusting updates**

This approach enables organizations to use a set national scale for all employees instead of individualized rates. For positions or talent that are critical, they may adjust the scale upward and offer higher salaries. This way, the employees working from rural and affordable locations will not have very low salaries, and the company can retain critical talent at a higher level of compensation. Zillow, an online real estate company, adopted this approach in order to remain competitive in the present reality.

HOW ARE COMPENSATION AND BENEFITS CHANGING?

Pay, however important, is only one piece of the compensation and benefits puzzle. Good, competitive salaries help businesses acquire and retain the right talent. When transitioning into remote and hybrid work models, the total rewards (beyond just the pay package) matter. One employee expectations survey found that around 65% of employees are willing to take a pay cut to work remotely, provided they are assured of additional benefits like flexible hours, more paid days off, etc.

While companies would consider remote work itself a benefit, it is not. It is just a work model. Remote workers need good healthcare, insurance, and other contextual benefits that matter to them. This will nurture positive employee experiences, boost their productivity and morale, improve their retention, and much more.

TRADITIONAL PERKS THAT AREN'T RELEVANT ANYMORE

In remote and hybrid models, some traditional benefits and incentives are irrelevant. Travel and commuter allowances, on-site childcare facilities, on-site gyms and fitness classes, social events, parking allowances, weekly catered lunches, free snacks and beverages in the office, and so on are all irrelevant for remote workers. These perks apply exclusively to in-office workers and not remote workers. Accordingly, several companies have removed these incentives from their total rewards packages.

Even in companies with hybrid work models, offering benefits tied to the office premises may cause resentment and disparities between those who can and cannot claim these perks. This will have a lasting, long-term impact on the work culture and employee engagement levels between remote and on-site workers.

WHAT NEEDS TO MAKE ITS WAY INTO COMPENSATION AND BENEFITS?

The above-mentioned perks have lost their appeal (even to in-office workers) because the pandemic raised several challenges for employees and questions for employers. The dire state of work-life balance, declining mental health, absenteeism, lower productivity, and high churn rates owing to increasing child and elder care burdens (especially among women employees) have necessitated the reshaping and reprioritizing of benefits.

Based on the lessons from the pandemic and the current priorities, here is a list of five incentives and perks that must make their way into an organization's restructured compensation and benefits.

1. Health and Wellness Benefits Including Mental Health

Organizations must prioritize the overall health and well-being of all employees. Investments in employee health and wellness show employees that the organization cares about them. Good physical, mental, and emotional health of employees is crucial to drive productivity and business value.

Access to telehealth, mental well-being, wellness apps, and so on through a unified employee wellness platform is one effective way. Since on-site gyms and fitness classes aren't an option for remote workers, companies need to provide access to virtual fitness classes, fitness apps, etc., to all employees and encourage them to engage in physical fitness activities.

Companies could also negotiate deals with gyms and fitness studio chains for their employees to take memberships from their location. Companies could also create fitness challenges and health tasks for all employees to accomplish every day. Participation can be improved in such activities by incentivizing employees through games, gift cards, leaderboards, etc.

To foster mental health and well-being among all employees, companies must provide access to counselors and therapists while destigmatizing mental illnesses. They should provide employees with the necessary resources to understand and improve their overall well-being. Apart from this, they could also invest in mental wellness, meditation, and other apps.

Further, companies could show employees that they care about them and their families by extending health and wellness schemes to families.

2. Flexibility and Work-Life Balance

One of the biggest challenges faced by remote workers is that they feel the pressure to be always on, always-available. This impacts their work-life balance adversely. Through flexibility, this problem can be addressed, and employees can be safeguarded from excess stress and burnout.

Flexibility is offered in a number of ways. For instance, flexi-timings help employees to schedule work, life, and play in a convenient manner. Reset days where employees can take a day off to recharge themselves are also growing in popularity. Google recently rolled out this benefit for its employees.

Flexible time-off is another way to offer greater flexibility to employees. The pandemic has shown how unpredictable life can be and how even well-laid plans can go haywire overnight. Flexible time-off enables employees to take time-off whenever they need it without any formal limit on it. Some companies are even offering unlimited paid time-off to employees. Managers would still approve the time-off and pull up employees for poor performance.

A data analytics firm, Fair Isaac Corp., is now offering a non-accrual-based vacation policy that is trust-based, instead of the traditional policies that require employees to earn their time-off and use it within the accrued limits.

Companies could also offer designated work from anywhere periods. So, employees can work from anywhere across the globe or take what is known as 'workcation'.

Another way to extend flexibility is by offering more home leave instead of sick days. This helps employees to take on some work on days they are sick but good enough to be able to get work done.

3. Robust Insurance Plans for the Employees and Their Families

This is non-negotiable in today's day and age, especially after the kind of havoc wreaked by the pandemic. Organizations must extend insurance plans to remote workers and their families. Insurance assistance could include health insurance, life insurance, disability insurance, and even pet insurance. Given the growing incidence of data breaches, identity thefts have become common today. So, some companies are even considering identity theft insurance.

Organizations can connect service providers with employees and negotiate discounted/subsidized premiums for insurance.

4. Child Care Benefits

Owing to socio-cultural norms and stereotypes, women remain the primary caregivers in their households, be it – childcare, elder care, or caring for an ill family member. Over the past 2 years, we have seen a large proportion of women employees and women leaders have been leaving the workforce for care work. The severe lack of work-life balance and domestic support for care work are contributory factors. This is why childcare benefits are critical.

Childcare benefits are offered through access to professional babysitting services, daycare allowances, access to engaging online classes, paid time-off, etc. Some companies also offer elder care benefits.

5. Incentives For Redesigning Home Office

Regardless of whether employees are working remotely or in the office, they need good equipment, a proper office setup, and a good work environment to be productive and innovative. So, companies are offering support to remote workers to create such an enabling environment. Some companies provide home office stipends while others offer allowances to purchase good equipment. Some companies also offer incentives to help employees create/redesign their home office.

OTHER BENEFITS COMPANIES ARE PROVIDING

- Home Care Services
- Subscription to streaming services and entertainment platforms

- Virtual events for socializing with co-workers
- Deals and discounts through negotiation with third-party vendors

MOVING FORWARD...

Keeping all employees, regardless of their location, goes a long way in keeping them happy, engaged, and productive. Choosing the right benefits is the way forward in the uncertain and complex future of work. Have you started the process of redesigning your compensation and benefits to keep pace with the current needs and context?

16. Innovate or Suffocate: The Lean Transformation

In the early 2000s, Pune was an emerging hub for technology and innovation, with a unique blend of youthful energy and a rich academic tradition. Anika, a brilliant computer science graduate, had always nurtured a dream of making a mark in the tech world. She saw the untapped potential of Pune and decided to harness its resources to build something extraordinary.

With limited resources but boundless determination, Anika rented a small, sunlit apartment overlooking the bustling streets of Pune. She gathered a team of passionate engineers, handpicked from her alma mater. They shared her vision of creating innovative software solutions that would not just meet market demands but exceed them. Their first office was a modest space filled with mismatched furniture and the constant hum of brainstorming sessions. The atmosphere was charged with the palpable excitement of a group of dreamers eager to make a difference.

THE LEAN BEGINNINGS

Anika and her team were disciples of lean principles from the outset. They embraced the philosophy of doing more with less, seeking efficiency, and staying laser-focused on delivering value. Failures were celebrated as learning experiences, and customer feedback was a cherished treasure. With a humble budget and a lean team, they were able to pivot quickly in response to market changes. Their products were not just software; they were manifestations of innovation and dedication. PuneTech Innovations swiftly gained a reputation for its ability to adapt, innovate, and deliver products ahead of schedule.**

**In those early days, employees wore multiple hats, working late nights and weekends, fueled by their passion for the company's mission. The culture was one of camaraderie, with everyone invested in the success of the venture.

THE BUREAUCRATIC QUAGMIRE

As PuneTech's reputation grew, so did its client base and the complexity of its projects. It was a period of both opportunity and challenge. Anika, in her pursuit of maintaining control and quality, began to introduce layers of processes and approvals. She believed that these would ensure that the company's growth was sustainable and its products reliable. However, the unintended consequence of these changes was a creeping bureaucracy. What were once quick, agile decisions turned into cumbersome deliberations. The innovative spirit that had fueled PuneTech's rise was slowly being buried under the weight of policies and procedures.

THE EPIPHANY

One fateful monsoon evening, PuneTech's transformation began. Anika found herself caught in a torrential downpour on her way to a meeting, a meeting that epitomized the growing red-tapism within the company. Instead of discussing a critical product strategy, the meeting had devolved into an endless debate over internal processes. Drenched and exasperated, Anika realized that PuneTech was on the cusp of losing the very essence that had set it apart. She knew that something had to change, and it had to start with her.

THE TRANSFORMATION

The days that followed were a whirlwind of introspection and action. Anika called for an emergency meeting with her leadership team. In the dimly lit conference room, she shared her vision of a leaner, more efficient organization that could respond swiftly to market dynamics. She emphasized the need for inbuilt checks and controls that streamlined decision-making without stifling creativity.

The leadership team, recognizing the gravity of the situation, rallied behind Anika's vision. It was a pivotal moment, a collective awakening to the fact that they needed to rediscover the entrepreneurial spirit that had powered their early successes.

THE RESULTS

PuneTech's transformation bore fruit swiftly. Projects that had previously languished in bureaucratic limbo now raced toward completion. Customer feedback became the compass guiding product development, resulting in solutions that resonated more deeply with the market.

Clients, who had once grown frustrated with the sluggishness of the organization, were now delighted by PuneTech's responsiveness and innovation. The company's reputation soared, attracting new clients and expanding its market reach.

THE CULTURAL SHIFT

The cultural shift within PuneTech was as profound as the transformation of its processes. Employees felt a renewed sense of ownership and purpose. They embraced the opportunity to make meaningful decisions and contribute to the company's success.

Anika's leadership style evolved from micromanagement to mentorship. She became a guiding light, fostering an atmosphere of trust and collaboration. The once-dreaded meetings transformed into dynamic forums for problem-solving and ideation. Walls of hierarchy crumbled, and employees from diverse backgrounds and skill sets came together to drive innovation.

THE RIPPLE EFFECT

Word of PuneTech's remarkable transformation spread like wildfire within Pune's tech community. The company became a beacon of hope for other startups and tech firms grappling with similar challenges. They saw PuneTech as living proof that an organization could balance control and agility, bureaucracy and innovation.

PuneTech became a magnet for top talent in the city. Skilled professionals from across Pune were eager to join an organization that prized both speed and stability. Pune's tech ecosystem embraced PuneTech's story as an exemplar of what could be achieved when an organization rediscovered its entrepreneurial spirit.

THE CONTINUED JOURNEY

Years rolled on, but PuneTech's commitment to lean principles and continuous improvement remained unwavering. Their growth was steady, characterized by a sustainable and purpose-driven approach. PuneTech had learned that innovation was not a one-time event but an ongoing journey.

Anika, now a respected figure in Pune's tech scene, became an advocate for a balanced approach between control and agility. She shared PuneTech's journey in numerous conferences and workshops, inspiring others to embark on similar transformations.

THE LEGACY

In the annals of Pune's tech history, PuneTech Innovations left an enduring legacy. They proved that, even in the face of growth and success, an organization could retain its entrepreneurial spirit by embracing lean principles and fostering a culture of empowerment. PuneTech's story served as an enduring inspiration to countless other startups and tech firms in Pune, all aspiring to achieve the same blend of innovation and growth that had defined PuneTech Innovations.

And so, in the heart of Pune's vibrant tech ecosystem, the story of PuneTech Innovations continued to inspire and shape the future of entrepreneurship. It remained a testament to the enduring power of lean thinking, the importance of striking a balance between control and agility, and the unwavering belief that innovation would always lead the way.

17. Navigating Layoffs with Empathy: A Manager's Tale

THE MORNING OF DIFFICULT DECISIONS

In the bustling city of Mumbai, Pristine Tech Solutions stood tall as one of the leading IT companies in India. The company was known for its innovative solutions, cutting-edge technology, and, most importantly, its talented team. Yet, even the most successful companies can face challenging times, and Pristine Tech Solutions was no exception.

The morning sun cast a warm glow on the glass façade of the office building as employees hurriedly made their way to their workstations. However, for Arjun Mehta, the hiring manager at Pristine Tech Solutions, this day held a heavy burden. The company had recently encountered some unexpected financial difficulties, forcing them to make a heartbreaking decision—laying off a significant portion of their workforce.

Arjun had spent countless sleepless nights pondering over the impending layoffs, knowing full well that these decisions would affect not just the livelihoods of his team members but also their hopes, dreams, and families. It was a responsibility he didn't take lightly.

As Arjun walked through the bustling office, he couldn't help but notice the vibrant atmosphere that had always characterized Pristine Tech Solutions. Teams huddled together in brainstorming sessions, colleagues exchanged laughter and ideas, and the constant hum of productivity filled the air. Today, however, the air was laden with a sense of unease.

THE WEIGHT OF RESPONSIBILITY

Arjun had prepared himself for a long and emotionally taxing day. He meticulously reviewed the list of employees who would be affected by the layoffs, taking into account their contributions to the company, their personal circumstances, and their aspirations. It was crucial to him that these decisions, as painful as they were, were made with empathy and consideration.

One by one, Arjun called each affected employee into his office. The moments leading up to those conversations were fraught with tension. Colleagues whispered worriedly to one another, and the sound of stifled sobs emanated from the closed office doors.

Among those affected was Ravi Kumar, a dedicated software engineer who had been with the company for over five years. He had come to Mumbai from a small village in Bihar to pursue his dreams and provide a better life for his family. Ravi was not just an employee; he was the sole breadwinner for his family, which included his aging parents and younger siblings.

As Ravi entered Arjun's office, his apprehension was evident. He took a seat across from Arjun, his hands trembling. Arjun cleared his throat and began to explain the situation. The words weighed heavily on him as he watched the color drain from Ravi's face.

Ravi listened intently, his mind racing as he contemplated how he would support his family without a stable job. Arjun could see the fear and anxiety in Ravi's eyes, and it tore at his heart.

Next up was Sneha Kapoor, a brilliant project manager who was expecting her first child in just a few weeks. Sneha had been a pillar of strength for her team, and her dedication to her work was commendable. Arjun had always admired her resilience and leadership qualities. As he delivered the news, Sneha's eyes filled with tears, and she instinctively clutched her pregnant belly. She thought about the uncertainty that lay ahead, not just for her but for her unborn child and her husband, who had been eagerly preparing for their baby's arrival.

As the day wore on, Arjun found himself sitting across from many more employees, each with their own unique stories and struggles. There was Vikram, a talented graphic designer who had always been a source of inspiration for the entire team. Vikram had poured his heart and soul into every project, and his dedication had been unparalleled. Arjun couldn't help but feel a profound sense of sadness as he delivered the news to Vikram. The dreams of a promising career and the aspirations he had nurtured were shattered in an instant.

THE RIPPLE EFFECT

As Arjun continued to deliver the news to each affected employee, he could see the anguish on their faces. He tried his best to offer words of encouragement and support, promising to provide references and assistance with job searches. But he knew that it would never be enough to ease their pain entirely.

The news of the layoffs spread like wildfire throughout the office. Friends consoled friends, colleagues hugged one another tightly, and the once-vibrant atmosphere of Pristine Tech Solutions was now tinged with sorrow and uncertainty.

One of the most challenging aspects for Arjun was the knowledge that these layoffs would not just affect the employees themselves but would send ripples through their families and communities. In India, the concept of "family" extends far beyond the nuclear unit. It encompasses parents, siblings, cousins, and even close friends. The burden of providing for an extended family can be immense, and Arjun knew that the weight of his decision would be felt by many.

A MANAGER'S GUILT

By the time Arjun had spoken to all the affected employees, he felt emotionally drained. The weight of the decisions he had just communicated hung heavily on his shoulders. He stepped into his office, closed the door, and leaned against it, tears welling up in his eyes.

The guilt gnawed at him. He questioned whether there was more he could have done to prevent this situation. He wondered if there were alternative solutions that he hadn't explored thoroughly enough. The pain of delivering such life-altering news to people he had worked closely with for years was overwhelming.

Arjun realized that he needed some form of emotional healing himself. He decided to seek professional help to cope with the emotional toll that came with delivering such difficult news. He enrolled in therapy, recognizing that it was crucial not only for his own well-being but also for his ability to continue supporting his team and the company.

REBUILDING LIVES

Over time, the affected employees began to pick up the pieces of their lives. Ravi, the software engineer, found a freelance project that helped him provide for his family temporarily. Sneha welcomed her baby with the support of her loving husband and parents, and she vowed to continue pursuing her career once her child was a bit older. Vikram, the graphic designer, started working on his own projects, slowly rebuilding his career and regaining the confidence that had been shaken by the layoffs.

Despite the pain of the initial shock, many of the laid-off employees discovered newfound strengths and talents within themselves. They realized that adversity could bring out the best in them. Some even embarked on entrepreneurial ventures, channeling their skills and creativity into building their own businesses.

LESSONS IN COMPASSION

In the end, the layoff decision was necessary for the survival of Pristine Tech Solutions. The company had weathered the storm and, with a smaller but more agile team, was back on its feet. Yet, the scars from that fateful day still lingered, not just for Arjun but for everyone involved.

Arjun had learned that sometimes, as a manager, you have to make tough decisions for the greater good of the organization. However, that doesn't make the process any less emotionally taxing. It had taken a toll on him, and he was grateful for the therapy that had helped him cope with the guilt and sadness he had felt for having to let go of dedicated and hardworking employees.

In the world of business, compassion and empathy should never be forgotten. Arjun vowed to carry these lessons with him to ensure that any future decisions, no matter how challenging, were made with a deep understanding of the human impact they would have.

EMPLOYEES – COMPETENCIES AND ASPIRATIONS

18. Navigating the First 90 Days: A Guide for Senior Leaders in the Heroic Journey

Welcome, brave senior leaders, to the exhilarating world of your new role! As you step into this superpowered adventure, it's essential to navigate the first 90 days with finesse and flair, ready to tackle the challenges and make a remarkable impact. So, grab your capes and get ready to embark on a comprehensive guide that will help you soar to success!

THE FIRST 90 DAYS: A JOURNEY OF TRANSFORMATION

As a senior leader, the first 90 days are a critical period of transition and transformation. It's a time when you establish your presence, build relationships, gain insights, and set the stage for your future leadership. By following these key principles, you can lay a solid foundation for success:

Understand the Context: Before diving headfirst into your new role, take the time to understand the organizational context. Familiarize yourself with the company's history, vision, mission, values, and strategic goals. Gain insights into the industry landscape, market trends, and competitors. This knowledge will serve as a compass for your decision-making and guide your actions as you lead your team forward.

Connect and Communicate: Forge alliances and build relationships with your team members, peers, and key stakeholders. Effective communication is the bedrock of successful leadership. Engage in one-on-one conversations, team huddles, and informal encounters to connect with individuals on a personal level. Seek to understand their perspectives, aspirations, and concerns. By building authentic relationships, you'll foster trust and collaboration and create a formidable team that can conquer any challenge.

Listen and Learn: Activate your superhuman listening skills and become a master of understanding. Embrace the power of active listening, where you absorb information from various sources and seek diverse perspectives. Be genuinely curious about the experiences and insights of your team members and stakeholders. Decode the organizational culture, values, and dynamics to navigate through potential obstacles and leverage opportunities. Empower your team members to share their insights, ideas, and concerns openly. Harness the collective wisdom of your allies, drawing inspiration from their experiences, to shape your leadership approach and make informed decisions.

Assess and Evaluate: To lead effectively, you must understand the strengths, weaknesses, and potential areas for improvement within your team. Unleash your analytical prowess to evaluate and optimize team performance. Assess the skills, capabilities, and dynamics of your team members. Dive deep into existing processes, projects, and resources, using your super-sleuthing skills to identify hidden talents, skill gaps, and opportunities. Armed with this knowledge, you can make informed decisions and assemble a mighty team ready to overcome any obstacle.

Set Clear Expectations: Illuminate the path to success by setting clear expectations for your team. Paint a vivid picture of the team's goals, priorities, and performance standards. Communicate the vision and strategy in a way that inspires and engages your team members. Ensure that everyone understands their roles, responsibilities, and the collective mission. By creating crystal-clear expectations, you'll guide your team, ignite their passion, and pave the way for heroic achievements.

Craft a Strategic Plan: Tap into your strategic genius and embark on an epic journey with your team. Develop a visionary plan that aligns their efforts with the organization's goals. Define bold initiatives, set milestones, and establish metrics to measure progress. Enlist the support of key stakeholders, forging alliances that will fuel the team's heroic endeavors. Lead your team toward a future where success is not just a possibility but a certainty.

THE DO'S: SUPERPOWERS FOR SUCCESS

To maximize your impact as a senior leader, there are specific actions and behaviors you must adopt. These "superpowers" will help you navigate the challenges, inspire your team, and achieve extraordinary results:

Forge Alliances: Unleash your superpowers of relationship-building! Take the time to connect with your team members, peers, and key stakeholders. Engage in captivating conversations, team huddles, and informal encounters that reveal their deepest aspirations, goals, and obstacles. By building authentic relationships, you'll foster trust, collaboration, and a formidable team ready to tackle any challenge.

Embrace the Power of Listening!: Activate your superhuman listening skills! Absorb information, seek diverse perspectives, and decode the organizational culture, values, and dynamics. Empower your team members to share their insights, ideas, and concerns. Harness the collective wisdom of your allies, drawing inspiration from their experiences to shape your leadership approach. By listening attentively, you can make informed decisions and build a culture of inclusivity and innovation.

Illuminate the Path: Shine a beacon of clarity on the road to success! Set clear expectations for your team. Paint a vivid picture of the team's goals, priorities, and performance standards. Ensure that everyone understands their roles, responsibilities, and the collective mission. Crystal-clear expectations will guide your team, ignite their passion, and pave the way to heroic achievements.

Harness the Power of Assessment: Unleash your analytical prowess and assess the team's strengths, weaknesses, and potential areas for improvement. Evaluate existing processes, projects, and resources with your super-sleuthing skills. Identify hidden talents, skill gaps, and opportunities to optimize performance. Armed with this knowledge, you'll make informed decisions and assemble a mighty team ready to conquer any obstacle.

Craft Your Strategic Odyssey: Tap into your strategic genius and embark on an epic journey! Develop a visionary plan for your team, aligning their efforts with the organization's goals. Define bold initiatives, set milestones, and establish metrics to measure progress. Enlist the support of key stakeholders, forging alliances that will fuel the team's heroic endeavors. Lead your team toward a future where success is not just a possibility but a certainty.

THE DON'TS: PITFALLS TO AVOID

While there are critical actions to take as a senior leader, there are also pitfalls to avoid. Be mindful of these common mistakes that can hinder your effectiveness and derail your journey:

Resist the Urge to Leap Before You Look: Hold your horses, valiant leader! Avoid the temptation to rush into drastic changes. Take the time to understand the existing processes, culture, and dynamics. Appreciate the heroes who have come before you and the wisdom they possess. By proceeding with caution, you'll earn the respect of your team and maintain stability during times of transition.

Honor the Wisdom of the Collective: Embrace the extraordinary talents within your team! Avoid dismissing ideas or undervaluing the expertise of your allies. Respect their knowledge and experience, valuing their contributions as you harness their collective brilliance. Foster an environment where collaboration and innovation thrive and where every hero's voice is heard.

Maintain the Balance of Promises: Beware the allure of overpromizing and underdelivering! Set realistic expectations based on a deep understanding of the organization's resources and capabilities. Avoid the pitfalls of making grandiose commitments that may backfire. Instead, focus on consistent progress, ensuring that your actions align with your words. By building a reputation for reliability, you'll earn the trust and admiration of your team.

Embrace Feedback, Defeat Resistance: Stand strong in the face of resistance and embrace feedback with valor! Welcome diverse perspectives, even if they challenge your initial plans. Engage in courageous conversations, seeking to understand the concerns and motivations behind resistance. Adapt your strategies with transparency and empathy, transforming skeptics into allies.

Unleash Your Inner Social Butterfly: Avoid the perils of isolation, mighty leader! Embrace your role as a beacon of inspiration and guidance. Interact with your team by participating in team activities, meetings, and events. Show your commitment to their success and foster a sense of belonging. By being present and accessible, you'll create a superheroic culture of collaboration and trust.

CONCLUSION: SOAR TO UNPRECEDENTED HEIGHTS

As you embark on your heroic journey as a senior leader, remember to build relationships, listen and learn, set clear expectations, assess and evaluate, and craft a strategic plan. Simultaneously, avoid rushing into changes, cherish the wisdom of your team, deliver on your promises, embrace feedback, and remain connected to those you lead. Armed with these insights, you're equipped to soar through the first 90 days with unwavering courage, leaving a lasting legacy in your organization. Now, go forth and unleash your heroic potential!

19. Harmonious Horizons: Redefining Work-Life Balance

In the vibrant city of Mumbai, where dreams and aspirations met the frenetic pace of life, a remarkable workplace called TechSolutions India stood as a beacon of innovation and inclusivity. Within its walls, the concept of work-life balance unfolded in countless variations, each reflecting the diverse backgrounds and unique circumstances of its employees.

BEGINNINGS

TechSolutions India was founded by Aditi Sharma, a visionary entrepreneur who believed that a company's success lay not only in its profits but in the well-being of its employees. She had a dream of creating a workplace where people from all walks of life could flourish and find equilibrium between their professional and personal lives.

The company's journey began with Aditi herself, a mother of three who had managed to build a successful career while nurturing her family. Her experiences as a working mother fueled her passion for creating a workplace that understood the delicate dance between work and life.

THE HEART OF THE COMPANY

At the heart of TechSolutions India was its dedicated HR team, led by Maya, a seasoned HR director with a deep commitment to employee welfare. Maya had a knack for recognizing the diverse needs of the workforce and tailoring policies to address them.

Maya believed that work-life balance wasn't a one-size-fits-all concept. She understood that it could take on different forms, from flexible hours to remote work options and even mentorship programs for employees with unique circumstances.

THE SINGLE PARENT'S STRUGGLE

One of the earliest challenges TechSolutions India faced came in the form of Sunita, a 35-year-old single mother of two young children. Sunita had been struggling to find a job that allowed her to fulfill her career ambitions without compromising her responsibilities as a parent.

TechSolutions India recognized Sunita's unique situation and offered her a tailored solution. They provided her with flexible hours and on-site daycare facilities, ensuring that she could excel in her role as a project manager while also being present for her children.

Sunita's story became a testament to the company's commitment to supporting employees in their journey toward work-life harmony. Her colleagues admired her resilience and the company's forward-thinking approach.

THE SENIOR'S ENCORE CAREER

In a country where retirement often meant a complete exit from the workforce, TechSolutions India introduced the concept of an "encore career." Vijay, a 62-year-old retiree with a passion for writing, found himself embarking on a second career as a content creator for the company's blog.

TechSolutions India's commitment to embracing talent regardless of age allowed Vijay to stay mentally active, engage with younger colleagues, and share his wealth of experience. He became an inspiration to others in the company, proving that age should never be a barrier to professional growth.

BREAKING STEREOTYPES

TechSolutions India actively challenges gender stereotypes in the workplace. Meera, a 30-year-old engineer, broke barriers in a predominantly male industry. The company not only offered her equal opportunities but also encouraged her to participate in leadership programs and provided mentorship.

Meera's story shattered glass ceilings and paved the way for other women in the field. She became a role model for aspiring female engineers, proving that gender should never limit one's potential.

THE MILLENNIAL ENTREPRENEUR

Among the employees was Arjun, a 26-year-old millennial with a fervent entrepreneurial spirit. While working at TechSolutions India, Arjun was also nurturing a side business venture. The company recognized his ambition and offered the flexibility he needed to balance his job and his entrepreneurial dreams.

TechSolutions India's support allowed Arjun to flourish in both his roles. He contributed effectively to the company while also pursuing his entrepreneurial aspirations, exemplifying how a progressive workplace could empower individuals to achieve their diverse goals.

THE COMPANY'S EVOLUTION

As the stories of Sunita, Vijay, Meera, and Arjun intertwined with those of Rohan and Aisha, TechSolutions India evolved into a pioneering workplace that celebrated diversity, inclusivity, and adaptability.

The company's commitment to creating a harmonious work environment that catered to the unique needs and circumstances of its diverse workforce began to garner attention. TechSolutions India was recognized as an exemplar of progressive work culture not only in Mumbai but across India.

THE RIPPLE EFFECT

As TechSolutions India continued to thrive and serve as a beacon of innovation and inclusivity in Mumbai's corporate landscape, its influence extended far beyond its walls. The stories of Sunita, Vijay, Meera, Arjun, Rohan, and Aisha, along with the progressive work policies of the company, created a ripple effect that touched the lives of countless individuals and transformed the way businesses and employees approached work-life balance in India.

A CULTURAL SHIFT

TechSolutions India's unwavering commitment to work-life balance has triggered a cultural shift in Mumbai's corporate world. Other companies began to take notice of the company's success and the positive impact its policies had on its employees' lives. They realized that fostering an environment that accommodated the diverse needs and circumstances of their workforce was not just a noble goal but also a competitive advantage.

The city, known for its relentless pace, started witnessing a gradual but significant transformation. Businesses across various industries began revisiting their work policies, recognizing that a more flexible and inclusive approach could lead to higher employee satisfaction, increased productivity, and enhanced talent retention.

THE RISE OF PROGRESSIVE WORKPLACES

Inspired by TechSolutions India's approach, several organizations across Mumbai began adopting progressive work policies. They introduced flexible working hours, remote work options, and mentorship programs to address the unique needs of their employees. The shift wasn't limited to tech startups; it encompassed a wide range of industries, from finance to manufacturing.

Aditi Sharma, the visionary founder of TechSolutions India, became a sought-after speaker and consultant, sharing her insights and experiences with other business leaders. Her advocacy for policies that supported employees in their quest for balance resonated with companies of all sizes and sectors.

EMPOWERING WOMEN IN THE WORKFORCE

One of the most significant impacts of TechSolutions India's progressive approach was the empowerment of women in the workforce. Meera's story of breaking gender stereotypes and thriving in a male-dominated industry had a profound influence on other women aspiring to pursue careers in technology and engineering.

TechSolutions India actively collaborates with organizations dedicated to gender equality and diversity. Together, they launched initiatives to mentor and support women in tech, providing them with the tools and opportunities they needed to succeed. The city witnessed a surge in the number of women entering STEM fields, and Mumbai began to make strides toward gender parity in the workplace.

THE AGING WORKFORCE AND ENCORE CAREERS

The concept of an "encore career" for senior employees, as exemplified by Vijay's second act as a content creator, gained traction across industries. Companies recognized the wealth of knowledge and experience that older employees brought to the table and actively sought to engage them.

In response, Mumbai saw a rise in opportunities for seniors to continue contributing to the workforce after retirement. This not only provided financial stability for retirees but also helped companies tap into a valuable resource of wisdom and expertise.

NURTURING ENTREPRENEURIAL DREAMS

Arjun's story of balancing his role at TechSolutions India with his entrepreneurial aspirations sets a precedent for other young professionals. The city witnessed a surge in side businesses and startups led by individuals who were empowered by their employers to pursue their passions outside of their primary jobs.

TechSolutions India collaborated with local entrepreneurship networks and incubators, further fueling the startup ecosystem in Mumbai. The city became a hub for innovation and entrepreneurship, attracting talent and investment from across the country.

ADITI SHARMA'S LEGACY

Aditi Sharma, the driving force behind TechSolutions India's progressive work culture, continued to advocate for the harmonious integration of work and life. Her vision had not only transformed a single workplace but had also sown the seeds of a cultural revolution that celebrated the importance of balance.

Aditi's journey inspired her to establish the "Work-Life Harmony Foundation," a nonprofit organization dedicated to promoting the adoption of progressive work policies in businesses across India. The foundation offered resources, guidance, and mentorship to companies looking to create more inclusive and flexible workplaces.

THE FUTURE OF WORK-LIFE HARMONY

As the years passed, the transformation of Mumbai's corporate landscape became a model for other cities and regions across India. The nation recognized the significance of embracing diversity, inclusivity, and adaptability in the workplace.

The term "work-life balance" evolved into "work-life harmony," reflecting a more holistic and integrated approach to life and work. Companies across India, from metropolitan centers to rural areas, began reimagining their work policies to accommodate the diverse needs of their employees.

TechSolutions India, having set the stage for this cultural shift, continued to thrive as a symbol of what was possible when a company prioritized the well-being of its employees. It remained at the forefront of innovation and inclusivity, always ready to adapt to the evolving needs of its workforce.

THE CLOSING ACT

In the heart of Mumbai, amidst the ceaseless hustle and bustle, individuals from all backgrounds, ages, genders, and circumstances found themselves not just employees but integral participants in a movement that celebrated their uniqueness. TechSolutions India's journey was a testament to the idea that work-life harmony was not a distant ideal but an attainable reality.

The city had embraced the notion that work and life were not separate entities to be balanced but interconnected facets of a fulfilling existence. Mumbai had become a city where individuals could pursue their passions, nurture their families, and excel in their careers without compromise.

Aditi Sharma's legacy lived on, as a guiding light for those who believed in the transformative power of a progressive workplace. Mumbai had not only rewritten its corporate narrative but had also set an example for the world, proving that, in the grand tapestry of life and work, there was a place for every shade, every story, and every individual striving for harmony.

20. Office Gossip: The Career Killer You Should Avoid

Engaging in office gossip can be tempting, as workplace dynamics and interpersonal relationships can sometimes lead to the spread of rumors, speculations, and negative conversations about colleagues. However, it is important to recognize that participating in office gossip can have significant negative consequences for your career and overall work environment. In this retort, we will explore in detail why engaging in office gossip is generally discouraged and how it can hamper your professional growth.

Damage to Professional Reputation: When you engage in office gossip, you risk damaging your professional reputation. **Gossip often involves spreading rumors or talking negatively about others, which can lead to a loss of trust and respect from your colleagues and superiors**. Your reputation is a valuable asset in your career, and once it is tarnished by participating in gossip, it can be challenging to rebuild. Employers value employees who are trustworthy, and discreet, and maintain confidentiality. Engaging in gossip can be seen as a lack of professionalism and judgment, which may result in missed opportunities for growth and advancement.

Erosion of Trust and Collaboration: Trust is a vital component of effective teamwork and collaboration. **When you participate in office gossip, it undermines the trust others have in you.** Colleagues may perceive you as someone who cannot be trusted with sensitive information or as someone who lacks discretion. This erosion of trust can hinder effective collaboration, as team members may hesitate to share their thoughts, concerns, or ideas with you. Additionally, when gossip becomes prevalent in the workplace, it creates a toxic environment where employees are more focused on personal conflicts and negative discussions than working together toward common goals.

Negative Impact on Workplace Morale: Gossip has a significant impact on workplace morale. When negative conversations and rumors circulate, it creates a culture of negativity that affects everyone involved. **Gossip breeds conflict, sows seeds of mistrust, and creates divisions among colleagues. Employees who are constantly subjected to gossip may feel anxious, stressed, or demotivated, which can lead to decreased productivity and engagement.** A toxic work environment not only harms individual employees but also impacts the overall organizational culture. When employees are focused on gossip rather than their work, it becomes challenging to foster a positive and supportive atmosphere that encourages collaboration and growth.

Legal and Ethical Implications: Engaging in gossip can also have legal and ethical implications. Sharing sensitive or confidential information about colleagues or spreading false rumors can lead to legal repercussions and damage the organization's reputation. Many workplaces have policies regarding the proper handling of confidential information, and violating these policies can result in disciplinary action or even termination. Furthermore, participating in gossip goes against ethical standards of professionalism, respect, and integrity. **It is important to uphold ethical principles in the workplace, treating others with fairness, honesty, and empathy. By avoiding gossip, you demonstrate your commitment to ethical behavior and build a reputation as someone who can be trusted to act with integrity.**

Fostering Positive Relationships and a Healthy Work Environment: Instead of engaging in office gossip, it is crucial to focus on building positive relationships and fostering a healthy work environment. By taking proactive steps, you can contribute to a positive workplace culture and enhance your professional growth.

1. **Practice Open and Respectful Communication**: Foster open lines of communication with your colleagues and superiors. Encourage transparent discussions, active listening, and constructive feedback.

2. **Cultivate a Supportive Network**: Build relationships based on trust, respect, and mutual support. Surround yourself with colleagues who uplift and inspire you and reciprocate the same positivity.

3. **Lead by example**: Be a role model for professionalism and integrity. Avoid participating in gossip and demonstrate that you prioritize respectful and positive interactions with others.

4. **Address Conflict Appropriately**: When conflicts arise, focus on resolving them in a constructive and respectful manner. Engage in open dialogue, seek understanding,

and work toward finding solutions that benefit all parties involved.

5. **Support a Culture of Recognition and Appreciation**: Acknowledge and celebrate the accomplishments of your colleagues. Express gratitude, offer praise, and foster a culture of appreciation that recognizes and values the contributions of every team member.

Instead of indulging in gossip and communication, focus on fostering positive relationships, practicing open and respectful communication, and promoting a healthy work environment. By doing so, you not only safeguard your career but also contribute to a more productive, supportive, and inclusive workplace where everyone can thrive. **Remember, the true mark of a professional is not the ability to spread rumors, but the capacity to build trust, inspire collaboration, and uplift those around them.** So, let's leave the gossip behind and create a workplace culture where respect, integrity, and growth take center stage.

21. Learning to Say No: Mastering the Art of Tactful Refusals

In the bustling heart of Delhi, where tradition and modernity coexisted in a harmonious cacophony, there lived a dedicated and seasoned manager named Rahul. Over the years, Rahul had meticulously climbed the corporate ladder of a prominent IT firm, achieved commendable milestones, and earned a reputation for his exceptional leadership skills and unrelenting work ethic. He was respected by his peers, admired by his subordinates, and trusted by his superiors. Rahul was, by all accounts, the epitome of a successful manager.

However, as his career ascended to new heights, Rahul found himself facing a growing dilemma—a dilemma that many managers eventually encounter. The demands of his managerial role seemed to be in a perpetual state of expansion, and he was incessantly being asked to take on additional tasks and responsibilities. It was as if his plate was never empty; instead, it felt like a bottomless pit that absorbed every request, every project, and every commitment that came his way.

At first, Rahul succumbed to the allure of saying yes to every request. He believed that being a team player meant always being available to help, and he didn't want to disappoint anyone. His commitment to delivering excellence and his desire to support his colleagues led him down a path where "yes" became his default response.

But as weeks turned into months, Rahul began to notice the toll this incessant agreement was taking on his well-being. His workload had become an ever-expanding universe, and he was struggling to navigate its complexities. He was overwhelmed, perpetually stressed, and, ironically, his once-stellar productivity was beginning to show signs of wear and tear. The very dedication and commitment that had propelled him to his managerial position were now threatening to push him to the brink of burnout.

Rahul's realization that something needed to change marked the beginning of a profound transformation in his managerial journey. He understood that saying yes to every request, every project, and every commitment was not sustainable. It was unsustainable not only for his own well-being but also for the quality of his work and his ability to lead effectively.

Rahul recognized that learning to say no was not a sign of being dismissive or uncooperative; instead, it was an essential skill for setting boundaries, prioritizing his workload effectively, and ultimately, achieving a sustainable work-life balance.

As he embarked on the path of mastering the art of saying no, Rahul realized that there were several critical lessons to learn, each of which played a pivotal role in his journey:

1. Be Honest and Clear: The first step Rahul embraced was the need, to be honest, and clear about his reasons for saying no. He understood that vague or ambiguous

responses often led to misunderstandings and unmet expectations. Therefore, he committed to being candid and straightforward when declining requests. If he didn't have the time, resources, or expertise to take on a new project, he communicated this clearly, avoiding any unnecessary ambiguity.

2. Show Empathy: Saying no, Rahul learned, was not just about protecting his own interests; it also involved showing empathy and understanding toward those making the requests. He acknowledged the significance of the request and the needs of the person asking for his assistance. Simultaneously, he explained why he was unable to fulfill the request. By demonstrating empathy, he maintained positive relationships and minimized the potential for conflicts or misunderstandings.

3. Use "I" Statements: In situations where Rahul had to decline a request, he realized the importance of using "I" statements instead of "YOU" statements. This subtle shift in language made a significant difference. Instead of making it seem like a judgment on the requester, Rahul framed his response in a way that highlighted his own limitations. For instance, instead of saying, "You're asking too much of me," he would say, "I don't have the bandwidth to take on this project right now." This approach made the conversation less confrontational and more focused on his own capacity.

4. Offer a Counteroffer: Rahul understood that there were instances where he couldn't fulfill a request in its entirety. In such cases, he considered offering a counteroffer. For

example, he might propose completing a portion of the request or assisting in a different way that aligns with his current commitments. This approach demonstrated his willingness to help while still maintaining his boundaries.

5. Practice Saying No: Like any skill worth mastering, Rahul recognized that saying no effectively took practice. He started small by declining minor requests that wouldn't significantly impact his workload. This allowed him to become more comfortable with the process and build his confidence. Over time, he gradually worked his way up to larger and more significant requests. Throughout this journey, he reminded himself that saying no was not a sign of weakness; rather, it was a sign of self-awareness and prioritization.

6. Don't Over-Explain: While it was important to be honest and clear about his reasons for saying no, Rahul was mindful of the potential pitfall of over-explaining. He understood the balance between providing adequate justification and delving into unnecessary detail. He aimed to stick to the main points and be concise in his communication. Over-explaining, he realized, could inadvertently open the door to negotiation, which he wanted to avoid.

7. Stay Firm: Perhaps one of the most critical lessons Rahul internalized was the importance of staying firm once he had said no. He recognized that giving in and saying yes after initially declining a request could send mixed messages and erode his credibility. Staying true to his decision was crucial not only for maintaining his work-life balance but also for upholding his integrity as a leader.

As Rahul began to implement these strategies in his professional life, he noticed a gradual but significant shift in his work-life balance and overall well-being. He felt a renewed sense of control over his workload, and the constant stress that had become his unwelcome companion began to dissipate. His productivity, once on the decline due to the burden of excessive commitments, rebounded and reached new heights.

Moreover, Rahul's team appreciated his newfound clarity and balance. They saw a manager who could effectively manage his own priorities, set boundaries, and make informed decisions about where to allocate his time and energy. Rahul's ability to say no when necessary didn't diminish their respect for him; instead, it enhanced it. They recognized him as a leader who prioritized the team's collective goals and well-being, even if it meant declining some individual requests.

Over time, Rahul's journey and transformation in the heart of Delhi became a source of inspiration to his colleagues and peers. His story served as a compelling reminder that, in a world characterized by relentless demands and constant connectivity, learning to say no was not a sign of weakness but a testament to one's ability to prioritize, manage workload effectively, and maintain a healthy work-life balance.

As Rahul continued to master the art of saying no, he discovered that it was not merely a skill but a profound act of self-care and leadership. By learning to decline certain commitments, he had gained the capacity to fully invest himself in those that truly mattered. He had achieved a balance that allowed him to excel in his managerial role, nurture positive relationships, and safeguard his own well-being—a balance that would undoubtedly serve him well in the ever-evolving landscape of the corporate world.

22. Courage in the Cubicles: A Workplace Transformation Tale

In the heart of Bangalore's thriving IT sector, Priya had carved out a promising career for herself. She was a talented software engineer at "TechNova Solutions," a company that was making waves in the industry. Her days were filled with coding, brainstorming sessions, and the camaraderie of her colleagues. Her future in the company seemed bright, and she was proud of her accomplishments.

However, as with any story of growth, challenges soon emerged that threatened to derail her trajectory.

THE UNSETTLING SHIFT

It all began with Rajat, her manager. At first, his actions were subtle, easily dismissed as friendly banter. But as days turned into weeks, Priya began to notice a disconcerting shift in his behavior. Rajat would often strike up conversations by the coffee machine, his remarks increasingly personal, filled with innuendos that made her uncomfortable.

During team meetings, he started making inappropriate sexual jokes, casting lewd glances in her direction as if testing the waters. The atmosphere in the room grew tense, and Priya's discomfort was palpable. She knew this wasn't normal workplace behavior, and she couldn't simply ignore it.

THE UNWANTED INVITATIONS

The situation escalated further when Rajat started extending invitations to Priya that went beyond the confines of the office. It started innocently enough with suggestions for coffee, framing it as an opportunity to discuss project details outside the work environment. Priya, hesitant but not wanting to seem uncooperative, accepted a few times.

But soon, the invitations grew bolder. Priya found herself receiving requests for dinners at upscale restaurants, all under the pretext of work-related discussions. The discomfort was now undeniable. Priya knew she had to take action to protect herself.

SETTING BOUNDARIES

As Priya pondered her next move, she decided to assert her boundaries. She had always been known for her professionalism, and she wasn't about to let anyone jeopardize her career. The next time Rajat invited her out for dinner, she took a deep breath and said, "I appreciate the offer, Rajat, but I prefer to go home and spend time with my family after work."

Rajat was momentarily taken aback by her assertiveness. He stammered for a moment but eventually nodded in understanding and backed off. Priya had set her first boundary, making it clear that her personal time was off-limits.

MAKING IT EXPLICIT

However, Priya soon realized that setting boundaries alone might not be enough. Rajat's behavior continued to push the envelope.

The inappropriate comments during meetings persisted, and the invitations, though less frequent, didn't cease entirely.

Priya knew it was time to be even more explicit. One day, after Rajat made yet another inappropriate remark during a team meeting, Priya decided to address it head-on. She looked him in the eye and said, "Rajat, I appreciate working with you professionally, but I want to be clear that I am not interested in pursuing any romantic or sexual relationship. Let's keep our relationship strictly professional."

It was an uncomfortable conversation, to say the least. Priya could feel the tension in the room, but she also felt a sense of relief after saying what needed to be said. Rajat seemed taken aback, but he nodded in agreement.

DOCUMENTING THE BEHAVIOR

Despite Priya's clear communication, Rajat's inappropriate behavior didn't stop. In fact, it seemed to intensify. Priya realized that she needed to take her protection a step further. She began documenting every incident meticulously.

She maintained a journal where she noted the date, time, and details of what was said or done during each encounter with Rajat. She also kept copies of any inappropriate messages or emails he sent. Priya knew that having a record of these incidents would be crucial if she needed to take further action.

REPORTING TO HR

As the days went by and Rajat's behavior persisted, Priya felt increasingly trapped. She understood that she couldn't handle the situation on her own. It was affecting her work, her peace of mind, and her overall well-being. She realized she had to escalate the matter.

Priya mustered the courage to report Rajat's behavior to the HR department at TechNova Solutions. She knew that her company had a policy in place for handling sexual harassment and inappropriate behavior in the workplace. It was a nerve-racking step, but Priya knew it was necessary.

The HR team took her complaint seriously. They assured her that they would conduct a thorough investigation into the matter. Priya felt a mix of emotions - fear, relief, and a glimmer of hope that the situation might finally be addressed.

SEEKING SUPPORT

The process of reporting the behavior was emotionally draining for Priya. She felt isolated and vulnerable, unsure of how her colleagues would react. In this difficult time, she decided to confide in a trusted colleague, Ananya.

Ananya had been a supportive friend at the company, and Priya knew she could trust her. She shared her ordeal with Ananya, who listened empathetically and provided Priya with a much-needed support system. Ananya assured Priya that she was not alone in this battle and encouraged her to stay strong.

Outside of work, Priya also leaned on her family for emotional support. Their unwavering love and encouragement gave her the strength to face the challenging days ahead.

THE COMPANY'S RESPONSE

As the investigation into Rajat's behavior progressed, it became evident that his actions were indeed inappropriate. The evidence

Priya had meticulously documented, coupled with testimonies from other team members who had witnessed his behavior, painted a clear picture.

TechNova Solutions took immediate action. Rajat was given a final warning, and Priya was moved to a different team to ensure her safety and comfort. The company also initiated sensitivity training programs to raise awareness about appropriate workplace behavior. Priya's ordeal had prompted positive change within the organization.

CONSIDERING A NEW PATH

However, despite the corrective measures taken by the company, Priya realized that she still didn't feel entirely safe or comfortable at TechNova Solutions. The trust had been broken, and the toxic environment had left a lasting impact on her. She knew she had to prioritize her well-being above all else.

After much contemplation, Priya decided to consider finding a new job. She viewed this as a fresh start, where she could once again thrive in a professional environment, free from harassment and discrimination. She couldn't change the past, but she could shape her future.

A NEW BEGINNING

As Priya settled into her new job at a different IT firm in Bangalore, she felt a renewed sense of empowerment. She knew that she had taken the right steps to protect herself and her career. She had set boundaries, made it clear that she was not interested, documented the behavior, reported it to HR, sought support, and ultimately decided to find a new job.

She understood that everyone had the right to work in a safe and respectful environment, and she had taken action to safeguard that right. Her journey was far from easy.

23. Confronting Toxicity: A Tale of Workplace Transformation

In the bustling heart of Mumbai, where skyscrapers stretched toward the heavens and the city's ceaseless energy pulsed through the veins of every street, there was a young woman named Aisha. She had always heard the age-old saying, "People don't leave companies; they leave managers." It was a sentiment often echoed by her fellow colleagues during their coffee breaks, a truism that seemed to hang in the air like the humidity of a Mumbai summer. But as clichéd as it might be, Aisha couldn't help but wonder if there was more truth to it than she had previously believed.

Aisha had been working at BrightSolutions, a digital marketing firm in the heart of the city, for three years. During that time, she had seen a parade of managers come and go, each one more challenging to work with than the last. She was beginning to wonder if her experience was unique or if this was just the way things were done in the Indian corporate world.

First things first, Aisha reminded herself of one sweltering morning as she sipped her chai and gazed out at the sea of people hustling on the streets below. You're not crazy, and you're not being unreasonable. If you have a gut feeling that you have a bad boss, you're most likely not wrong.

As Aisha reflected on her journey at BrightSolutions, she couldn't help but think about the several signs she had read about that indicated a toxic, insecure, or frustrating manager. Her current boss, Mr. Kapoor, seemed to embody many of these signs.

- Your manager doesn't let you do your job – It had been months since Aisha had been allowed to complete a project without Mr. Kapoor's constant interference. Every time she attempted to take initiative, she was met with resistance or told that her ideas were not worth pursuing.

- Your ideas are constantly turned down – Aisha had a notebook filled with innovative marketing ideas and strategies. But whenever she presented them to Mr. Kapoor, he brushed them aside, preferring to stick with outdated methods.

- Your manager never offers constructive feedback – Aisha was eager to learn and improve her skills, but Mr. Kapoor's idea of feedback was a vague nod or, worse, complete silence.

- Your manager never notices or acknowledges your accomplishments – Despite receiving praise from colleagues and clients for her hard work, Mr. Kapoor rarely acknowledged her achievements. In fact, he often downplayed her successes or claimed credit for them himself.

- Your manager only focuses on the numbers, not the people – Metrics were the sole focus in their department, and Mr. Kapoor cared more about meeting revenue targets than the well-being of his team. Requesting time-off was met with skepticism, and personal lives were considered a hindrance.

- You're expected to be perfect, with zero room for error – The fear of making a mistake hung over Aisha like a dark cloud. Mr. Kapoor's lack of clear expectations turned every task into a potential minefield.

- Your manager has to approve of every single thing you do – Aisha often felt like a marionette, with Mr. Kapoor pulling the strings. Every project, email, and decision had to be run by him for approval.

- You're constantly left out – Aisha was often excluded from important meetings and opportunities that could help her career grow. She was expected to excel but was never given the chance to prove herself.

- Your boss doesn't take your job seriously – Mr. Kapoor once openly questioned the value of Aisha's role, making her feel like she had to constantly justify her place in the company.

- Your manager is rude – Condescending and disrespectful remarks were a daily occurrence. Passive-aggressive emails disguised as feedback left Aisha feeling small and demoralized.

- Your manager criticizes or talks negatively about other people in front of you – Aisha winced as Mr. Kapoor tore into colleagues, finding fault in everything they did. He often expected her to join in and agree with his criticisms.

- You're asked to do things outside of your moral character – Requests for unethical actions left a knot in Aisha's stomach. She refused to compromise her integrity, even if it meant going against her boss's wishes.

- You're expected to figure things out on your own – Aisha rarely saw or spoke to Mr. Kapoor, except when he needed something. Whenever she asked questions, he looked annoyed and impatient.

Aisha knew she couldn't continue like this. It was clear that Mr. Kapoor was a toxic presence in her professional life, and it was taking a toll on her overall well-being. She needed to take action, but it wouldn't be easy. Leaving her job might seem like the obvious solution, but she had to consider her options carefully.

Depending on her specific situation, there might still be room to learn and grow at BrightSolutions despite her manager's behavior. If there were other benefits to staying, she wouldn't let Mr. Kapoor drive her away. People only had as much power over her as she allowed them to have, and unless her manager was jeopardizing her job security or career growth, she would find a way to navigate the challenges and rise above the chaos.

One evening, after a particularly frustrating day at work, Aisha decided to confide in her best friend, Raj. They had known each other since childhood, and Raj had always been the voice of reason in her life.

Over plates of piping hot pav bhaji at their favorite street-side stall, Aisha poured her heart out to Raj, sharing her experiences and frustrations with Mr. Kapoor.

Raj listened intently, his brow furrowing as he processed the litany of complaints. Finally, he took a deep breath and said,

"Aisha, I've known you for a long time, and I've never seen you this stressed and unhappy. It's clear that your boss is making your life miserable, and it's affecting your mental well-being. Have you considered talking to someone higher up in the company?"

Aisha sighed, swirling her chai in its glass. "I've thought about it, Raj, but I'm not sure if it would make a difference. Besides, I don't want to create unnecessary drama at work."

Raj nodded thoughtfully. "I understand your concerns, but sometimes you have to stand up for yourself. Toxic bosses thrive on the silence and fear of their employees. You're talented and hardworking, Aisha, and you deserve better."

Aisha appreciated Raj's support and advice. She knew he was right; it was time to address the issue. The next morning, she mustered the courage to schedule a meeting with the HR manager, Ms. Verma.

In the cozy, glass-walled HR office, Aisha recounted her experiences to Ms. Verma. She explained the challenges she faced and the toll it was taking on her mental health. Ms. Verma listened attentively, her expression growing increasingly concerned as Aisha spoke.

"I'm truly sorry to hear that you've been going through this, Aisha," Ms. Verma said empathetically. "No one should have to endure a toxic work environment. We take such matters seriously at BrightSolutions."

Aisha felt a glimmer of hope. "Is there something that can be done, Ms. Verma? I want to continue working here, but the situation with my manager is unbearable."

Ms. Verma nodded. "I appreciate your commitment to the company, Aisha. Let me speak with the senior management team and see if we can find a solution to address this issue. In the meantime, I'll encourage you to document any incidents or interactions with your manager that make you uncomfortable. It will help us build a case if needed."

Aisha left the HR office with a renewed sense of hope. She began keeping a detailed journal of her interactions with Mr. Kapoor, noting dates, times, and the nature of each encounter. It was a therapeutic exercise that allowed her to regain a sense of control over her situation.

Days turned into weeks, and Aisha continued to work diligently while documenting her experiences. She noticed that Mr. Kapoor's behavior became somewhat more cautious as if he sensed that something had changed. It was a small victory, but it gave her a glimmer of hope.

One sunny afternoon, Ms. Verma called Aisha into her office for a follow-up meeting. Aisha entered nervously, unsure of what to expect.

"Please, have a seat, Aisha," Ms. Verma said with a warm smile. "I wanted to update you on the situation regarding your manager. After a thorough review of your documentation and discussions with senior management, we have decided to take action."

Aisha's heart raced with anticipation. "What kind of action, Ms. Verma?"

"We have decided to provide Mr. Kapoor with leadership training and coaching," Ms. Verma explained. "We believe that with the right guidance and support, he can improve his managerial skills and create a healthier work environment for his team."

Aisha was relieved to hear this news. While she had initially contemplated leaving her job, she realized that she had invested a significant part of her career at BrightSolutions. If there was a chance to bring about positive change, she wanted to be a part of it.

Over the next few months, Aisha noticed gradual improvements in Mr. Kapoor's behavior. He began to offer constructive feedback, acknowledge her accomplishments, and involve her in important meetings and projects. It was as if the toxic cloud that had hung over the team was slowly dissipating.

As Aisha's working conditions improved, she decided to take it upon herself to mentor younger colleagues who were facing similar challenges. She shared her experiences and offered guidance on how to deal with difficult bosses. Aisha realized that by supporting others, she could help create a more positive work culture within the organization.

One day, as she was having lunch with a junior colleague, Priya, the young woman confided in Aisha about her own struggles with her manager, Mr. Joshi.

"It sounds like you're going through a similar situation that I faced with my previous manager," Aisha said empathetically. "But remember Priya, you're not alone, and you don't have to endure this silently."

Encouraged by Aisha's words, Priya decided to take action. She scheduled a meeting with Ms. Verma and shared her experiences and concerns about Mr. Joshi. Aisha offered her support, accompanying Priya to the meeting as a witness.

Ms. Verma, impressed by Priya's courage, assured her that the company would investigate the matter thoroughly. She recognized that the culture of the organization needed to change, and it was only possible through the collective efforts of employees like Aisha and Priya.

In the months that followed, BrightSolutions implemented a series of initiatives to foster a healthier work environment. Leadership training programs were extended to other managers, and an anonymous feedback system was established to encourage open communication.

As the changes took root, Aisha felt a renewed sense of pride in her workplace. She had witnessed firsthand how individuals, united in their determination to confront toxic behavior, could bring about positive transformation. It was a lesson that transcended her professional life and became a testament to the resilience and strength of individuals in the face of adversity.

In the midst of these changes, Mr. Kapoor, her once-toxic boss, had become a more considerate and effective manager. He expressed his gratitude to Aisha for helping him recognize the need for improvement. It was a humbling moment for both of them, a reminder that personal growth was possible even in the most challenging circumstances.

BrightSolutions, once plagued by toxic management practices, had begun to shine as a beacon of positive change in the corporate landscape. Aisha, Priya, and countless others had demonstrated that it was possible to challenge the status quo and create a workplace where employees were valued, respected, and empowered.

As Aisha looked out at the bustling streets of Mumbai, she couldn't help but feel a sense of satisfaction. She had not only overcome the challenges posed by a toxic manager but had also played a role in transforming her workplace into a more inclusive and supportive environment.

24. Toxic Manager's Fall: A Tale of Courage and Collective Action

In the bustling city of Delhi, where the heart of the nation's corporate world beat with ceaseless vigor, there was a renowned software company known as "InnoTech Solutions." For years, it had been a beacon of innovation and excellence, a place where dreams of technological advancement became reality. But as with any organization, it was not immune to the occasional storm that threatened its very core.

The storm in question arrived in the form of a new manager, Rajesh Verma. His appointment had been met with high hopes and expectations. With a stellar resume and a reputation for driving results, Rajesh was entrusted with leading a team of 25 members in the Research and Development department. His arrival carried with it the promise of progress and prosperity, but little did anyone know that beneath the surface, a tempest of toxicity was brewing.

At first, Rajesh's leadership seemed promising. He appeared charismatic and confident, a leader who could inspire his team to reach new heights. However, it didn't take long for the team members to realize that something was awry. Rajesh's leadership style was far from what they had expected; it was a toxic concoction of manipulation, deceit, and cruelty.

The toxicity began subtly, with Rajesh creating an atmosphere of fear and uncertainty. He would berate team members in front of their colleagues, publicly humiliating them for perceived mistakes. He had an uncanny ability to make even the most confident employees doubt their abilities, eroding their self-esteem bit by bit.

As the weeks turned into months, Rajesh's true nature became increasingly apparent. He manipulated data and reports to paint a bleak picture of his team's performance. Through cleverly crafted statistics, he portrayed his subordinates as bumbling incompetents, masking their genuine achievements and contributions. The atmosphere within the team grew more toxic with each passing day.

The toxicity didn't end with data manipulation; it extended to Rajesh's treatment of his team members. He developed a penchant for singling out the most sincere and hardworking employees, targeting them with ruthless precision. His tactics included overloading them with impossible workloads, assigning them menial tasks, and frequently changing their job roles to create confusion and frustration.

The impact on these sincere employees was devastating. They found themselves caught in a web of despair, unsure of how to escape the clutches of their ruthless manager. Some of them, worn down by relentless pressure and stress, reluctantly handed in their resignations. The team that had once thrived on dedication and passion is now disintegrating.

As if targeting sincere employees wasn't enough, Rajesh began to abuse his position in more sinister ways. He set his sights on the female employees in his team, making unwelcome sexual advances and creating a hostile work environment. Those who dared to resist his advances were subjected to subtle retaliation, as Rajesh maneuvered to have them eliminated from the company.

The toxic cloud that hung over Rajesh's team had become unbearable. The once-vibrant workplace now echoed with the hushed conversations of employees who shared their tales of suffering. The collective morale was at an all-time low, and the mental and emotional well-being of the team members was in shambles.

However, the toxicity didn't go unnoticed. Rumors began to circulate, not only within Rajesh's team but also among employees from other departments. The poison seeping from Rajesh's leadership had become a cause for concern that transcended team boundaries.

Conversations in the cafeteria and whispered discussions in hallways revealed the extent of Rajesh's toxicity. Concerned colleagues from various teams realized that they couldn't remain silent any longer. They knew that if they were to effect change, they needed to come together and take a stand against this reign of terror.

In a clandestine meeting held in a dimly lit conference room, representatives from different departments gathered to strategize. They discussed their shared concerns and the evidence they had gathered to support their claims. It was a risky endeavor, as they were well aware of the repercussions they might face for challenging a manager.

As they pored over the evidence, it became abundantly clear that Rajesh's behavior was not an isolated incident. It was a systemic issue that had infected the entire workplace. The group resolved to take their case to the higher echelons of the company.

The collective evidence was substantial and damning. It included records of harassment, data manipulation, falsified reports, and testimonies from victims of Rajesh's toxic behavior. The group compiled their findings into a comprehensive report, leaving no room for doubt about the extent of the problem.

With the evidence in hand, they decided to approach the higher management of InnoTech Solutions. Their goal was clear: to expose Rajesh's actions and demand accountability. It was a risky move, as they were well aware that it might lead to a direct confrontation with a manager who had already proven himself to be ruthless.

Their efforts did not go unnoticed. The higher management, alarmed by the evidence presented to them, recognized the gravity of the situation. They were acutely aware of their responsibility to protect their employees and the company's reputation. It was time to launch a thorough investigation into the allegations against Rajesh Verma.

The investigation was conducted with meticulous care, ensuring that every piece of evidence was examined closely. The testimonies of team members were heard, and their grievances were taken seriously. The company's commitment to a safe and healthy work environment was unwavering, and they were determined to uncover the truth.

As the investigation unfolded, the truth emerged like a beacon of light in the darkness. Rajesh Verma was found guilty of creating a hostile, toxic, and abusive workplace. The evidence was incontrovertible, and the consequences were swift and severe.

InnoTech Solutions wasted no time in taking decisive action. Rajesh Verma's employment with the company was terminated, and he was removed from his managerial role. The message sent by the higher management was clear: such behavior would not be tolerated, and the well-being of their employees was their highest priority.

The news of Rajesh's removal from the company spread like wildfire among the employees. The collective sigh of relief that swept through InnoTech Solutions was palpable. It was a testament to the power of collective action and the courage to stand up against toxicity in the workplace.

The damage caused by Rajesh's toxic reign was not easily undone. The scars left on the team members ran deep, and the healing process would take time. However, the company had taken a significant step toward recovery and renewal.

InnoTech Solutions emerged from the ordeal as a stronger, more resilient organization. The incident served as a stark reminder that the fight against toxicity required vigilance and collective action. The employees demonstrated that, when united by a shared purpose, they could bring about meaningful change and protect the values and principles that defined their workplace.

As the sun set over the sprawling city of Delhi, the employees of InnoTech Solutions knew that their journey was far from over. They had faced the darkness of toxicity head-on and emerged victorious. It was a testament to their resilience, their commitment to a safe workplace, and their unwavering belief in the power of collective action.

In the end, the story of InnoTech Solutions served as a beacon of hope, a reminder that even in the face of adversity, individuals could come together to effect positive change. The toxic manager had been removed, but the spirit of unity and the commitment to a healthy work environment remained stronger than ever.

25. Breaking Free from Career Sabotage: Embracing Your Path to Success

In the ever-evolving landscape of the professional world, individuals hold the power to shape their own career trajectories. However, it's not uncommon for individuals to unintentionally sabotage their own success through various behaviors and choices. From a lack of self-awareness to neglecting professional relationships, these career-sabotaging tendencies can hinder growth and the realization of one's full potential. In this article, we will explore some common ways in which people may inadvertently undermine their professional success. By understanding these factors, individuals can take proactive steps to avoid career self-sabotage and pave the way for a thriving and fulfilling professional journey.

LACK OF SELF-AWARENESS: THE BLINDSPOT BARRIER

A fundamental aspect of building a successful career is self-awareness. Failing to recognize one's strengths, weaknesses, and areas for improvement can lead to misguided choices, accepting ill-suited roles, or missing out on valuable development opportunities. By embracing self-reflection and seeking feedback, individuals can gain a deeper understanding of themselves and make more informed decisions to propel their careers forward.

POOR WORK ETHICS: THE MOTIVATION MELTDOWN

Consistently displaying a lack of motivation, commitment, or professionalism can undermine one's professional progress. Engaging in procrastination, frequent absenteeism, missing deadlines, or maintaining a negative attitude toward work can hinder productivity, erode trust, and limit opportunities for growth. Cultivating a strong work ethic and demonstrating dedication to excellence can lay the foundation for long-term career success.

INEFFECTIVE COMMUNICATION: THE CONNECTION CONUNDRUM

Effective communication is a cornerstone of professional growth. Poor communication skills, whether it's failing to listen attentively, conveying messages unclearly, or using inappropriate language, can impede collaboration, damage relationships, and hinder career advancement. By honing communication skills and fostering open and transparent dialogue, individuals can foster stronger connections, improve teamwork, and unlock new opportunities.

RESISTANCE TO CHANGE: THE INNOVATION IMPASSE

In today's rapidly evolving workplace, adaptability is paramount. Those who resist change, cling to outdated methods, or refuse to embrace new skills and technologies risk falling behind in a competitive landscape. By embracing a growth mindset, seeking continuous learning opportunities, and embracing innovation, individuals can position themselves as valuable assets in an ever-changing professional environment.

LACK OF NETWORKING: THE CONNECTION VOID

Building and nurturing a professional network is vital for career growth. Failing to invest in meaningful relationships with colleagues, mentors, or industry professionals can limit opportunities for collaboration, mentorship, and career advancement. By actively engaging in networking activities, participating in industry events, and cultivating genuine connections, individuals can tap into a vast pool of knowledge, support, and opportunities.

NEGLECTING CONTINUOUS LEARNING: THE KNOWLEDGE GAP

In today's dynamic job market, continuous learning is essential for career progression. Neglecting to invest in ongoing professional development can result in stagnant skills and outdated knowledge, rendering individuals less competitive in their field. By embracing a lifelong learning mindset, seeking out training programs, attending conferences, or pursuing certifications, individuals can stay ahead of the curve and position themselves for future success.

ETHICAL LAPSES: THE INTEGRITY IMPLICATION

Engaging in unethical behavior can have severe consequences for one's professional reputation and career trajectory. Acting dishonestly, cheating, or violating company policies erodes trust and integrity, potentially derailing even the most promising career paths. Upholding strong ethical principles, demonstrating honesty, and adhering to professional standards are crucial for building a solid foundation of trust and respect.

LACK OF SELF-ADVOCACY: THE VOICE VOID

Advocating for oneself in the workplace is essential for career advancement. Failing to speak up for accomplishments, express career aspirations, or negotiate for better opportunities can result in being overlooked for promotions, raises, or career-enhancing experiences. By asserting oneself confidently, articulating goals and ambitions, and actively seeking growth opportunities, individuals can position themselves for success and garner recognition for their achievements.

BURNING BRIDGES: RELATIONSHIP RIFTS

The professional world is interconnected, and building and maintaining positive relationships is vital for long-term success. Poorly managing relationships, engaging in conflicts, or leaving a trail of broken bridges can tarnish one's professional reputation and limit future opportunities. By practicing effective conflict resolution, fostering a collaborative mindset, and prioritizing building and nurturing strong connections, individuals can create a supportive network that propels their careers forward.

LACK OF GOAL ALIGNMENT: THE DIRECTION DILEMMA

Failing to align personal goals with the broader objectives of the organization can result in disengagement and a lack of motivation. Understanding the company's vision, mission, and goals and aligning personal aspirations accordingly ensures that individuals contribute meaningfully and find purpose in their work. By actively seeking opportunities that align with personal goals and aligning efforts with organizational objectives, individuals can fuel their career progression.

By recognizing these potential career sabotage factors, individuals can proactively address them and make conscious choices that align with their professional growth and success. Embracing self-awareness, fostering a strong work ethic, enhancing communication skills, embracing change, building a network, pursuing continuous learning, upholding ethics, advocating for oneself, nurturing relationships, and aligning goals are key steps in avoiding career self-sabotage and unlocking the full potential of one's professional journey. With determination, reflection, and a commitment to personal growth, individuals can navigate the professional landscape with confidence and achieve long-lasting success.

...The Final Cut.

In any organizational structure, employees can typically be classified into two broad categories: Individual contributors and managers. These two groups play pivotal roles in the growth and functioning of an organization. The contribution of individual employees, who are responsible for their specific tasks and projects, is instrumental in achieving the day-to-day operational objectives of the organization. On the other hand, managers have a distinct role in shaping the broader organizational culture and steering the strategic direction.

The significance of both individual contributors and managers cannot be overstated, but it's the managers who often hold the reins of influence when it comes to shaping an organization's culture. Their decisions, actions, and leadership style can greatly impact how employees perceive the company, their work environment, and their overall job satisfaction. It's in this context that the process of elevating an individual contributor to a managerial role becomes a critical aspect of organizational management.

The elevation from an individual contributor to a manager is a pivotal moment in an employee's career. It's not just a career advancement; it's a transition from being a specialist in a particular domain to overseeing and guiding others in that domain. Therefore, organizations need a robust and well-considered process for this transition.

Typically, this process involves a multifaceted evaluation of the individual's readiness to assume managerial responsibilities. Two primary parameters are often considered in this evaluation:

1. **Service Duration:** The tenure of an individual in the organization is a significant factor. Longer service duration often indicates a deeper understanding of the organization's culture, processes, and goals. It implies a commitment to the organization's mission and a history of contributing positively.

2. **Performance:** The individual's performance is a crucial metric. It's not merely about meeting expectations but consistently exceeding them. Exceptional performance demonstrates that the individual has a good grasp of their current role and responsibilities.

However, the process doesn't stop at these two criteria. Recommendations from current managers, mentors, or team leads often play a crucial role in the decision-making process. These recommendations shed light on the individual's interpersonal skills, ability to collaborate, and overall leadership potential.

While these criteria may seem reasonable, there's a significant gap in this process: the evaluation of an individual's competencies and capabilities to manage effectively. Often, the focus is disproportionately placed on tenure and performance, with less attention given to the question: Does this individual have the essential qualities, skills, and knowledge to manage others?

Becoming a manager requires a distinct skill set that encompasses communication, conflict resolution, decision-making, strategic thinking, and people management. It's not just about being good at one's job; it's about enabling and empowering others to perform at their best. Unfortunately, many organizations assume that a star performer in an individual contributor role will automatically excel as a manager. This is a critical oversight that can have profound implications for both the organization and the individual.

Promoting someone to a managerial role without adequate preparation can lead to various challenges. The new manager may struggle with team dynamics, delegation, giving constructive feedback, and aligning their team's efforts with the organization's goals. This can result in a toxic work environment, reduced employee morale, and potentially higher turnover.

Additionally, the transition from an individual contributor to a manager is not just about acquiring new skills; it often requires a fundamental shift in mindset. Individual contributors typically focus on their own work and objectives, while managers must prioritize the success of their team and the organization as a whole. This shift can be challenging, and without proper training and support, individuals may find themselves ill-prepared for their new roles.

So, how can organizations address this gap in the process? The answer lies in a structured approach to leadership development.

Leadership development programs, often referred to as "Leadership Pipeline" or "Management Training," are instrumental in preparing individuals for managerial roles. These programs are designed to equip high-potential employees with the skills and knowledge necessary to excel as managers. They typically include a mix of training, mentoring, and on-the-job experience.

These programs can be customized to suit the organization's unique needs and can address the specific competencies required for managerial success. They often cover areas such as communication skills, conflict resolution, decision-making, strategic thinking, people management, delegation, feedback, and performance management.

These leadership development programs are not a one-size-fits-all solution. They should be tailored to an individual's specific needs, and they should also be an ongoing process. Leadership development is not a one-time event; it's a continuous journey of growth and learning.

Additionally, organizations need to emphasize that not all-star performers will, or even should, become managers. Some individuals may excel in their roles as individual contributors and may not have the inclination or interest in taking on managerial responsibilities. It's crucial to provide growth opportunities for these individuals within their domain of expertise, such as specialized roles or individual contributor tracks.

In our professional journey, both Pavithra and I have had the privilege of working with a wide spectrum of managers. We've been fortunate to collaborate with inspiring leaders who have demonstrated exceptional leadership qualities, as well as some who, regrettably, exhibited poor management skills and even toxic behaviors. Our experiences have underscored the importance of not just having managers but having great managers. Great managers can motivate, guide, and inspire their teams, fostering a positive work environment where individuals thrive. On the contrary, poor managers can stifle creativity, hinder productivity, and create a toxic work atmosphere.

Recognizing the significance of this aspect, we embarked on a project to document our experiences and insights working with different types of managers. We aimed to share our observations, challenges, and success stories to shed light on what makes a manager truly effective and how they can contribute to the organization's success.

Due to space constraints and the sheer volume of experiences and stories to share, we've limited this book to a selection of anecdotes and insights. We understand that effective management is a vast and multifaceted subject that cannot be fully explored within the confines of a single book.

Our hope is that this initial collection of experiences will resonate with readers who have encountered a diverse array of managers throughout their careers. We believe that by sharing these stories and lessons, we can offer valuable insights and guidance for navigating the complexities of managerial relationships and responsibilities.

Our ultimate goal is to gauge the response to this book and determine if there's a demand for further exploration of this topic. Depending on the feedback and interest we receive, we plan to collaborate on two additional projects:

1. **A Guide for First-Time Managers**: This guide will provide a comprehensive roadmap for individuals making the transition from individual contributor to manager. It will cover essential skills, common challenges, and best practices to help new managers excel in their roles.

2. **A Workbook for Great Managers:** This workbook will focus on what it takes to become not just a good manager, but a great one. It will delve into advanced leadership concepts, effective strategies, and exercises to help current managers enhance their leadership skills and foster a positive and productive work environment.

Organizations must invest in leadership development programs to prepare their employees for the challenges and responsibilities of management. Additionally, they should acknowledge that not everyone needs to become a manager to progress in their careers, and alternative career paths should be readily available.

We hope that our book serves as a valuable resource for individuals navigating the complexities of the managerial landscape, and we look forward to the possibility of expanding our exploration of this topic in the future. Thank you for joining us on this journey of understanding and improving the world of management.